PURSUING HOLLYWOOD

Crossroads in Qualitative Inquiry

Series Editors
Norman K. Denzin, *University of Illinois, Urbana-Champaign*
Yvonna S. Lincoln, *Texas A&M University*

ABOUT THE SERIES

Qualitative methods are material and interpretive practices. They do not stand outside politics and cultural criticism. This spirit of critically imagining and pursuing a more democratic society has been a guiding feature of qualitative inquiry from the very beginning. The Crossroads in Qualitative Inquiry series will take up such methodological and moral issues as the local and the global, text and context, voice, writing for the other, and the presence of the author in the text. The Crossroads series understands that the discourses of a critical, moral methodology are basic to any effort to re-engage the promise of the social sciences for democracy in the twenty-first century. This international series creates a space for the exploration of new representational forms and new critical, cultural studies.

SUBMITTING MANUSCRIPTS

Book proposals should be sent to Crossroads in Qualitative Inquiry Series, c/o Norman K. Denzin, Institute for Communication Studies, 810 S. Wright Street, University of Illinois, Champaign, IL 61820, or e-mailed to n-denzin@uiuc.edu.

BOOKS IN THIS SERIES

Incarceration Nation: Investigative Prison Poems of Hope and Terror, by Stephen John Hartnett (2003)

9/11 in American Culture, edited by Norman K. Denzin and Yvonna S. Lincoln (2003)

Turning Points in Qualitative Research: Tying Knots in the Handkerchief, edited by Yvonna S. Lincoln and Norman K. Denzin (2003)

Uprising of Hope: Sharing the Zapatista Journey to Alternative Development, Duncan Earle and Jeanne Simonelli (2005)

Ethnodrama: An Anthology of Reality Theatre, edited by Johnny Saldaña (2005)

Contempt of Court: A Scholar's Battle for Free Speech from Behind Bars, by Rik Scarce (2005)

The Pull of the Earth: Participatory Ethnography in the School Garden, by Laurie Thorp (2005)

Writing in the San/d: Autoethnography among Indigenous Southern Africans, edited by Keyan G. Tomaselli (2005)

Performing Black Masculinity: Race, Culture, and Queer Identity, by Bryant Alexander (2006)

Pursuing Hollywood: Seduction, Obsession, Dread, by Nathaniel Kohn (2006)

PURSUING HOLLYWOOD

Seduction, Obsession, Dread

Nathaniel Kohn

A Division of
ROWMAN AND LITTLEFIELD PUBLISHERS, INC.
Lanham • New York • Toronto • Oxford

AltaMira Press
A Division of Rowman & Littlefield Publishers, Inc.
A wholly owned subsidary of The Rowman & Littlefield Publishing Group, Inc.
4501 Forbes Boulevard, Suite 200
Lanham, MD 20706
www.altamirapress.com

PO Box 317, Oxford OX2 9RU, UK

British Library Cataloguing in Publication Information Available

Library of Congress Cataloging-in-Publication Data

Kohn, Nathaniel, 1944–
    Pursuing Hollywood : seduction, obsession, dread / Nathaniel Kohn.
      p.   cm. — (Crossroads in qualitative inquiry)
    Includes bibliographical references and index.
    ISBN-13: 978-0-7591-0924-7 (cloth : alk. paper)
    ISBN-10: 0-7591-0924-9 (cloth : alk. paper)
    ISBN-13: 978-0-7591-0925-4 (pbk. : alk. paper)
    ISBN-10: 0-7591-0925-7 (pbk. : alk. paper)
    1. Kohn, Nathaniel, 1944– 2. Motion picture producers and directors—
United States—Biography. I. Title. II. Series.
PN1998.3.K64A3 2006
791.4302′32092—dc22

                                      2006001681

Printed in the United States of America

♾TM The paper used in this publication meets the minimum requirements of American National Standard for Information Sciences—Permanence of Paper for Printed Library Materials, ANSI/NISO Z39.48–1992.

For Pam, Sophie, and Lily
with love

Contents

Preface

If you so choose, you can read this book as a coming-of-age story for our times, an autobiographical regaling of my life in the movie business, a ramble out of innocence that slowly turns into an autoethnographical examination of a particular time and place in a familiar late twentieth-century landscape—a move from the personal to the social made inexorable because I take Stuart Hall's detour through theory and have trouble finding my way out. Or you can feign innocence yourself and read these pages as a simple narrative account of my sometimes obsessive, always ambivalent relationship with the culture industry, specifically the independent motion picture business, and my role as a writer-producer in that industry.

My intent, if I can be said to have any, is to make this book an insider's tale that confronts how movies get made, who gets chosen to make them, who is seduced into thinking she or he can make them, and who becomes obsessed with trying to make them. This book tells my story, a common narrative about someone who, like so many others, ends up in a state of perpetual desire, enveloped by those recurring forces that drive more and more people, blinded and helpless, yet eager and hopeful, toward Hollywood. It shows how I (and many of the people I encounter along the way) struggle to become and remain a part of it all—in the movies, on TV, a player at any level.

This book is my attempt to show how in my own life I struggle with and against these hegemonic formations and how the self-awareness borne of critical theory finally complicates, confuses, and confounds rather than clarifies. An example: I urge myself to say, but cannot now fully do so, at least not with confidence, that this book is about how I use autobiography not as "a mere reflection of self, but another entry point into history, of community refracted through self" (Visweswaran 1994, p. 137). Sounds good, huh? So I will say it, knowing now that "sounding good" is about all I can hope for.

Written as a linked series of minimalist short stories with continuing characters and omnipresent communication technologies, the chapters in this book seek to unravel a mystery in which I, the ostensible detective, become the ultimate victim. And in the course of this insider narrative—while I unwittingly chase the disembodied imperialistic Hollywood crook—I reveal in ways hitherto unseen to me the workings of the low-budget independent film business; through writing about my everyday life, me as exemplar, I work to expose the complex manner in which independents feed—and feed off—Hollywood's voracious consuming practices, showing how anyone anywhere (me included) can now easily find a tentacle of the beast to grab hold of.

On another plane, what you read here is about Stuart Hall's detour through theory, how my growing fascination with critical theory as encountered in the academy becomes in itself an obsession, a warping factor that is a dizzying labyrinth from which I can no longer find escape nor even reprieve. An emerging self-reflexivity generates this obsession that turns me into a willful accomplice in Baudrillard's perfect crime (the murder of reality)—the flaneur gets sucked in, mangled, never to be spit out.

Theory tickles me in the beginning, then seduces me, then corrupts me, then intertwines with my spine like a hungry vine. It starts out as an eager prism in my spectacles; I think myself blind without it, though I yet don't know what "it" is; and without awareness, I reach a point where everything is refracted through ever-increasing layers of complementing, competing, contentious, convoluting, voracious theory. And then the crazy becomes sane, the absurd logical, the ironical transparent (and vice versa), as foundations fall away, beliefs turn contingent, and contexts expand and contract and fold in and around themselves ad nauseam, like an electric sock in the hands of a shivering maniac.

And then it becomes more. Theory becomes something out of a cheap science fiction movie—the hungry vine mentioned above—much more than a map, or a prism, or a rhizome, or a structural (or poststructural) grid or maze of grids, much more even than a map of a maze of grids seen through a prism. Theory is finally organic, growing, out of control, like Jack's beanstalk, contorting my spine, mingling with it, mangling its structural delicacies, invading my senses, my muscles, my nerves, my desire, my ache, inspiring a kind of epistemological atrophy as it encourages psychasthenia, until I no longer need to know, nor to feel, nor to want, nor to dread, for I am dead to the world's realities, as I expand to fill all space for all time, no trace left behind, save for the Derridian stink of theory.

Then again, maybe not.

I can also say, guiltlessly, guilefully, even gratefully (and through that gradual introduction of critical, postmodern, and postcolonial theory as they are visited upon me and my desires), that this book seeks to elucidate a new dimension of the pervasive lure of Hollywood and its production apparatus. In the end, it becomes more than an autoethnographic account of me among culture makers and their wannabes (although it is that as well). What that "more" is, however, is not for me to say, but for you—the reader-detective—to mine and, perhaps, to use.

Here I use my brushes with the taunts and pursuits of fame to paint a picture, sometimes painful, sometimes joyous, of how people like me come to live our lives as something temporary, as waiters (in the true sense of the word) in a global postmodern Hamburger Hamlet, waiting to be discovered, waiting to be summoned, waiting to become a part of it all.

You might want to look on this book as a succession of linked vignettes that are stylistically influenced by the work of minimalist short story writers like Raymond Carver. With a couple of exceptions, the chapters herein are dialogue-intensive narratives that strive to "show" and not "tell," in the occasional hope that

Walter Benjamin might have approved. You will find little inter-
nal monologue or theoretical discussion outside dialogue (and
very little inside dialogue). However, as the narrative progresses,
the weight of theory begins to tug at my memories, first in subtle
ways and then more urgently and selfishly, as it affects perception,
behavior, and talk, a crescendo of dread, until I begin to resemble
Benjamin's angel of history:

> His face turned toward the past. Where we perceive a chain of
> events, he sees one single catastrophe that keeps piling wreck-
> age upon wreckage and hurls it in front of his feet. The angel
> would like to stay, awaken the dead, and make whole what has
> been smashed. But a storm is blowing from Paradise; it has got
> caught in his wings with such violence that the angel can no
> longer close them. The storm irresistibly propels him into the
> future to which his back is turned, while the pile of debris be-
> fore him grows skyward. This storm is what we call progress.
> (Benjamin 1968)

Or Hollywood. In the end, I fear, dread becomes me.

However, as I plod backward into the future, no matter where
I cast my gaze, the presentation—simple, jargon-free writing in
short story form—always remains the same, as I oscillate betwixt
and between Hollywood and the academy and their various men-
dacities, threats, and seductions (as I try to capture how lives are
performed and knowledge employed to achieve success in the
entertainment/information regime).

Occupying the spaces between these chapters, and sometimes
buried within them, are short quotations from theorists who
influence, ignore, challenge, tease, and interact with my text—
Trinh Minh-ha, Homi Bhabha, Jean Baudrillard, Walter Benjamin,
Charles Baudelaire, Eve Sedgwick, Norman Denzin, Rey Chow,
Georgio Agamben, Gloria Anzaldúa, Martin Amis, to name a few
of them. This juxtaposition of quotations with my various tales be-
trays a certain recklessness, even playfulness, which I take again
from Walter Benjamin and model on his ponderer/allegorist,
who reaches "now here, now there, into the chaotic depths that
his knowledge places at his disposal, grabs an item out, holds

it next to another, and sees whether they fit: this meaning to that image, or this image to that meaning. The result never lets itself be predicted; for there is no natural mediation between the two" (Buck-Morss 1989, pp. 241–42). Unpredictable and unsettling, I try to play with image, meaning, and form through such juxtapositions—in a struggle to bring, in the words of Raymond Carver, something new from my world to yours, even something new from my past to my present to my future.

And while working within the form of the short story, I struggle against that form, hoping to find not symmetry and closure, but polyphonic voices, diverse selves, and astounding juxtapositions. Mingling spare dialogical interactions with thick description and coincidental popular culture texts, I promote a lingering verisimilitude, a gift of sorts, that invites you to enter the world I am performing, this mess of words becoming for you, perhaps, a model for exploring your seductions, obsessions, and the dread and desire that inevitably confound us all.

Method of this work: Literary montage. I have nothing to say, only to show.

—Walter Benjamin, *The Arcades Project*

I have been working to change the way I speak and write, to incorporate in the manner of telling a sense of place, of not just who I am in the present but where I am coming from, the multiple voices within me.

—bell hooks, *Yearning*

To live in the unhomely world, to find its ambivalencies and ambiguities enacted in the house of fiction, or its sundering and splitting performed in the work of art, is also to affirm a profound desire for social solidarity: "I am looking for the join ... I want to join ... I want to join."

—Homi Bhabha, *The Location of Culture*

Prologue: Hail the Conquering Hero

Let me tell you how I once came to be a part of it all. And let me tell you as I might have told you then, before I thought much about telling, in a time when I read John Buchan and Eric Ambler and Graham Greene, in a time when I hungered after faraway places....

> I have a report from agents everywhere—peddlars in South Russia, Afghan horse-dealers, Turcoman merchants, pilgrims on the road to Mecca, sheikhs in North Africa, sailors on the Black Sea coasters, sharp-skinned Mongols, Hindu fakirs, Greek traders in the Gulf, as well as respectable Consuls who use ciphers. They tell the same story. The East is waiting for a revelation. It has been promised one. Some star—man, prophecy, or trinket—is coming out of the West. (Buchan 1916, pp. 18–19)

It is the mid-1970s, and I think I am not unschooled in the manner of the Third World. I have read of faraway places. I have seen and occasionally cursed Orientals in fifty-dollar cars as I negotiate the streets of the small university town I call home. I have been entertained in the salons of Europe and made polite conversation with Indians. I have paid the equivalent of fifteen cents to watch a donkey and a woman attempt sex in a shantytown barnyard outside Panama City, Panama.

None of that, though, prepares me for Africa, where I go as a motion picture producer, a naive and eager star out of the West.

Africa rises up to meet my plane. Africa—at first sight a strangely ordered swelling of the ground, yellow hills not unlike the lined and sagging breasts of Mother Earth herself. But not like them either, these brilliant mounds. For I soon discover they are traces of something modern, of frenetic digging, of white greed and black labor, of golden dreams coming true.

Johannesburg, a city that miners scratched out of the mile-high dirt only a century before, now the financial center of South Africa, is an uncertain metropolis that teeters on shafts of unremembered mines; yet she lies before me, her arms open wide, beckoning. Hail, she says to me, hail the conquering hero. For she knows that I come from Hollywood, that Hollywood is my Queen Isabella. Hail, I hear myself say, hail me.

Outside my guest quarters in a walled mansion in the white northern suburbs, where I roam fresh from Europe, any preconceptions I might have of "Africa" evaporate like so many drops of tropical rain on boiling hot tarmac. I find black faces outnumbering white by a dizzying percentage, yet I walk without fear, not thinking to compare my feelings with the anxieties that overcome me every time I descend the steps of the 63rd Street Station into the jungle of Chicago's South Side.

In the city center, Johannesburg presents me with a densely packed swarm of faces and a chorus of voices, out of tune, out of sync, not caring or knowing that it is so, as they knock against each other on crowded streets that teem with excitement, adventure, possibility. Or so it seems to me, as I manage simultaneously to plow through and float above the crowd, one of them, yet not, an outsider armed with the weapons of knowledge and a secret agenda, an adventurer come to forage and, with time, to conquer.

In John Vorster Square, I am somehow empowered by my otherness, a purposeful American with an air of casual slumming about me, and also by my sameness, for I soon discover these city streets hold humanity from everywhere, a few even from that place I call home. And it is my ears that tell me so, as much as my eyes, the mangle of words rubbing up uneasily against each other. There are, among others, Portuguese refugees from the wars in Angola and Mozambique, Xhosas from the Ciskei and the Transkei, Zulus from Ulundi and Durban, Britishers fleeing the civil war in Rhodesia, coloreds from the Cape, Afrikaners up for the day from farms in the Orange Free State, witch doctors selling their muti, German tourists glum at the unlikelihood of illicit sex, Russian Jews from current and past exiles, bankers from Chase Manhattan, lawyers from the NAACP, Swazis from KaNgwane, Indian peddlers, Tswanas from Bophuthatswana, stockbrokers in safari suits, legless beggars on skateboards, and me, an American movie producer.

I am overwhelmed by the energy. At the same time, I want to capture it and be a part of it, not caring, not thinking that such wishes are in most ways opposed, logically barely possible. I do not yet understand that happenstance has shown me a way into my wish image, a forbidden passage, a means by which I can accomplish the possibility—belonging to what I have captured. Unknowingly, I am about to enter into that process—I am going to arrest the phantasmagoria with film, in the movies, and make it real. I am going to remake it as I imagine it, with me as a part of it.

But first I have another job, the mission that brought me to this place, a quest for resources, services, and money to help finance the movie I want to produce. It is called *Zulu Dawn*, the story of the Battle of Isandhlwana, a bloody rout that took place on the morning of January 22, 1879, a fight to the death between 1,500 British soldiers and 25,000 Zulu warriors. It took the Zulus, armed only with spears and tactics, about forty-five minutes to massacre all but a handful of the British soldiers, in spite of the Imperial army's Enfield rifles, cannons, rockets, and bayonets. The screenplay is by Cy Endfield (no relation to the rifle) who also wrote, produced, and directed *Zulu* (1964), an award-winning epic starring Michael Caine, Jack Hawkins, and Stanley Baker. *Zulu Dawn* is intended as a kind of sequel and will eventually become known among the virtuosos of language as a "prequel."

As Cecil Rhodes did a century before me, I size up the wealth around me and send glowing dispatches to my associates, backers, and bankers in Europe. And like Bartle Frere and Lord Chelmsford in the *Zulu Dawn* screenplay (the bureaucratic and military architects of the invasion of Zululand), I fashion pleas for support out of vague truths I discover in and through my own imagination. Yet I feel justified; I know I am fully in the right in crafting such mendacious appeals, for I have seen the riches of the land and know, with the armies of the Western film industry at my side, I will generate success, wealth, and dominion for them and for me. All anybody needs is a little guidance. All I need to do is convey my enthusiasm.

Where Rhodes had the Rothschilds and Queen Victoria, I have International Asset Control (IAC) and International Creative Management (ICM). Of course, ITT (International Telephone and Telegraph, although its real business is anything but) is the model, one of the first aggressively high-profile multinational corporations, an employer of private armies, an inventor of that version of international finance that does things that are locally illegal but globally not-yet-regulated—finance moves faster than the law, always has, always will; that is how fortunes are made.

IAC and ICM are not in ITT's league, but they know a good model when they see it. IAC is a London-based company headed by an aggressive Englishman named Guy Collins who knows how to encourage people and banks to give him their money to invest and manage. IAC vets speculative ventures on a global scale, trades in options, futures, shares, and currencies, sets up offshore tax shelters and numbered accounts, owns shell companies in Liechtenstein and the Dutch Antilles, fashions consortiums of merchant banks from Rotterdam to Geneva to Hong Kong. ICM is the largest talent agency in the world with offices in LA, New York, London, Paris, and Rome. It controls major stars like Steve McQueen, Sean Connery, Burt Lancaster, and Barbra Streisand. And it is actively adding producers to its rolls of actors, writers, and directors. Out of its Paris office, headed by a suave Frenchman named David Raphael, ICM is moving into the sales agency business, courting producers by raising production funds through discountable territorial presales. ICM also does the banking of the contracts, takes commissions, and owns pieces of the project, its distribution, even its producers—all income flows through ICM, and always less flows out than flows in.

I brought IAC and ICM together to structure, finance, and sell the movie I wanted to make. I enticed them with the screenplay, with the success of the first *Zulu* in Great Britain, continental

Europe, and Australia, and with the promise of below-the-line finance (local costs, in part) from South Africa. That South African participation is what I am attempting to line up—my mission as I ascend the glass-and-steel towers that rise out of the hurly-burly of the Johannesburg streets.

That I never get hard cash from the English or the Afrikaans banks, that I never succeed in prying venture capital from the wealthy Europeans in the big houses with the high fences north of the city center, that I am not able to work money-moving schemes even among those Europeans foresighted enough to want to get out while the getting is good are all testaments to the sophistication of the South African financial community, to the more secure investment options available, and to the success of fly-by-night movie promoters who came before me. This failure on my part, which I couch in far different terms in my telexes and phone calls to Collins and Raphael, leads to more of the finance coming out of Europe and forces me back into the streets, to wheel and deal at the margins among those of color who do not have the means of international capital at their fingertips. I am obliged to deal with Indians and Zulus to save a few pennies, to give the budget an appearance of balance, and, ultimately, to make the movie happen.

The words come out mangled, as if forced through a meat grinder in his throat. "It is a distinct pleasure to be making your acquaintanceship, sir."

Shorty Mohammed is a plump, jolly Pakistani, a generation or two removed from the Indian subcontinent, who has only recently relocated to Johannesburg from Salisbury, where he was a taxi driver of some reputation.

We are drinking tea in the back room of an Indian clothing store at the International Bazaar a mile or so beyond the freeway that bounds central Johannesburg on the south and west. But we could easily be in Delhi or Algiers or Kampala or London or New York. That familiar mixture of sweet aromas, of cumin and saffron and jasmine and other exotics not known to me, makes the air in this close room sleepy with intrigue. Around us in this dark and windowless place are high piles of sun-faded yellow boxes, the flimsy tiny-corrugated cardboard torn to reveal brightly colored trinkets and cloth, fabrics of other lives in other places. I speak in hushed tones that befit the clandestine nature of our meeting, while Shorty booms and laughs and slaps his knee with an enthusiastic glee.

"It is not the money of myself I am talking about. It is the money of my cousin and some of the business people he is doing business with. I am, as you say, the go-between."

And so I make the arrangements with Shorty for an exchange of currencies—U.S. dollars for South African rand—at a rate 35 percent more favorable to me than any bank can offer. It will prove to be a complicated global transaction full of checks and balances, protections for both parties against each other and against the prying eyes and ears of the South African state security apparatus, who consider such transactions illegal.

The cousin of Shorty Mohammed owns an Indian restaurant near Joubert Park in the pulsating heart of Johannesburg, around the corner from the Landdrost Hotel, where I am staying in the Pineapple Suite—all the lamp bases are large, colorful porcelain pineapples, and the bedspread is emblazoned with a queen-sized abstracted pineapple. No real pineapples are anywhere in evidence.

At 9:00 a.m. on the appointed morning—we are already filming *Zulu Dawn* near Pietermaritzburg and need cash to pay about one thousand anxious Zulu extras—I leave the hotel lobby and push my way through the now familiar urban maze to the Star of India restaurant, a modest eatery marked only by a weathered sign on a tiny doorway under a wooden balcony that shades the crowded sidewalk. I knock three times, pause and knock four more times. Again the smell, this time laced with curry and tandoori and tobacco, as the door opens to darkness and I slip inside.

Shorty is not there, but his cousin Thom is, a small thin Pakistani with a moustache and the easy grace of a man grown accustomed to ushering diners to secluded tables. The restaurant is closed until dinner, but I see and feel other dark men in the shadows, most seated at tables covered in starched white linen. Smoke from incense and cigarettes floats up toward a single mud-smeared skylight. At the end of the shadowy and dreary room behind a small wooden table stands a very old man.

"My uncle," says Thom. "He has a small factory near Pretoria that makes samosas and other delicacies. He speaks Afrikaans but English no."

He bows. I do the same. In anticipation, I wipe my palms on my pants. But no hands are offered to shake, and I am afraid to offer mine.

On the table are two new cardboard suitcases lined with pastel-colored tissue papers, a pastiche of muted pinks and purples swaddling piles of South African rand notes that overflow onto the table. Also on the table is a single black telephone, tall and full of curves, a relic from a previous age. The number handwritten across the center of the dial is 22-22-22.

"You may wish to count the money," says Thom. "It is, as we agreed, totalling 425,000 rand."

I say that I'd better count it, that proper business procedure requires that I count it. The money is in ten-rand notes, the largest denomination in circulation. The faded and worn bills are fastened together with rusty paper clips, ten to a bunch, 4,250 bunches by my calculation. After a while, I give up counting individual notes and just count bunches.

It still takes me a long time. The Indians light cigarettes and wait. The air goes thick and pungent.

As I count, I wonder why the paper clips are rusty. Perhaps, I think, the money has come out of the ground, or out of cellars, or from mattresses in shacks with dirt floors, the life savings of desperate and trapped people.

Finally, I confirm the total and ask to use the phone. I direct-dial a number in London and listen to the rotary dial click out the digits, each in its own time. A familiar voice answers.

"Yes," I say loudly into the mouthpiece, "it is a gorgeous day in Johannesburg. . . . Wish you were here, too. . . . " I then ask Guy to call my sister and wish her a happy birthday, to tell her that "her present is in the mail." Then I say, "Don't forget." Then I add, "Do it right now."

I hang up the phone and nod at Thom and his uncle. The anonymous men at the edges of the room shuffle a little, their wooden chairs squeaking on the tiled floor.

"He is telexing the order to Geneva now," I say. "The money should be transferred within fifteen minutes."

The three of us look at the telephone.

"It is 4:30 in the a.m. in Boston," says Thom.

"Yes," I say.

The Habib Bank is in Boston, the branch we want, the one the money is being wire-transferred to. The sending bank, our bank, is the merchant banking arm of Indianapolis's American Palmer Bank. It is located in Geneva, Switzerland.

An hour passes. Then two...

"I will telephone them," says Thom. The uncle, now sitting, hands laced across his stomach, nods no. His eyes then move to me and stare.

Finally, shortly after noon the phone rings. Thom picks it up. He says yes three times, okay once, and good-bye.

His lips turn up at the edges in a kind of smile.

"It is there," he says, "187,000 U.S. dollars. In Boston, in America. Actually, it is 35 dollars short, but never mind."

"The transfer fee," I say. "Banks. You know what they are like. I told them—"

"We will waive it," says Thom. "And you may be keeping the suitcases, if you are wishing."

Hurriedly, although I work at feigning a certain deliberate calm, I close and fasten the cases. I say my good-byes and pick them up. They are extraordinarily heavy. As I make my way to the door, I feel a host of dark eyes upon me, and I have visions of some kind of double-cross, of something out of a John Buchan novel, a knife with a long curved blade being thrust between my shoulder blades, accompanied by the cry of "Infidel!" But I make it to the door unharmed, and Thom opens it for me, cautiously, peering outside before stepping aside.

"If you like," he whispers, "we can do it again."

"Perhaps," I say, "we can."

I step out into the brightness of day, the streets even more crowded now, a moving swaying sea of people of every color and every fashion, most of them now it seems watching my every move. Eyes down, I enter the stream with my two suitcases, anonymous cheap cardboard cases I keep telling myself, like any tourist carries. No one could possibly know of their contents.

Covered in sweat, I trudge the two blocks to the office of Joel Melamed, my South African lawyer. He waits to take me to the plane, a single-engine Piper that is on standby at a small runway on a farm just beyond Sandton. I must be on the location near Ulundi before dusk to pay the Zulus, to avoid possible riot.

Joel, a paunchy South African Jew whose family came to South Africa two generations ago, drives fast, his chest close to the steering wheel.

"From Mohammed to Melamed," he says, exaggerating his importance, as is his way. "Not such a far distance after all."

The undulating purple hills of Zululand roll unspoiled toward a distant horizon, a far cry from the babble and rabble of Johannesburg. This, I think as I watch the Zulus line up to collect their pay, is the real Africa, what Africa really means, the Africa I am capturing, a pastoral landscape of incredible solitude, unlike any other spot on earth, singular in its beauty, universal in its appeal. I am apprehending it (and the bloodbath that took place here in 1879), and I will return with it to the capitals of the West, to be hailed a conquering hero there (as well), where it matters most— in the pages of *Weekly Variety* and on the beaches at Cannes in the festival month of May.

Full of the twilight moment and its enveloping visions, I stand in the spreading darkness next to the accountant's table, as he and his assistant slowly remove the rusty paper clips and count out the rand notes. Under a small marquee behind me, Douglas Hickox, the director, and Burt Lancaster, who plays Colonel Durnford in the film, stand at a makeshift bar. They smoke cigarettes and sip martinis by candlelight, while in front of me, trailing away into the distance, the long lines of black bodies, faceless figures every one of them, wait patiently to collect their dues.

Enthralled, I watch as the thousand Zulus assume a deep purple aura in the red rays of the fast-setting sun. The colors are dense, thick, mystic as they dance with each other, eventually fusing into a boundless and impenetrable blackness. I think, this is all mine. I created this. I made it happen. I am here and now fully present in the world. I am a part of it all.

I hear Burt Lancaster laugh, that full unrestrained laugh that I remember so well from *Elmer Gantry*.

"Hey," he shouts to me. "Come in out of the cold and have a drink with us."

"I will," I say. "In just a minute."

Darkness is complete. The Zulus become the night, their presence betrayed only by the hum of their shuffling feet.

It is a magnificent moment, a moment never to be forgotten, a moment beyond words.

PART I

SEDUCTION

We must invent a new language, a new form of writing that goes beyond autoethnography, mystories.... This must be the language of a new sensibility, a new reflexivity, refusing old categories.... This new language, poststructural to the core, will be personal, emotional, biographically specific, minimalist in its use of theoretical terms. It will allow ordinary people to speak out and to articulate the interpretive theories that they use to make sense of their lives.... This language will be visual, cinematic, kaleidoscopic, rhizomatic, rich and thick in its own descriptive detail, always interactive as it moves back and forth between lived experience and the cultural texts that shape and write that experience.

—Norman K. Denzin, "The Lessons James Joyce Teaches Us"

Words too close to life *expose*. They share with the readers an intimacy that demands an equal laying bare and commitment on their part. "Placing one's self level with the body" in writing is, among other things, putting one's finger on the obvious, on difference, on prohibition, on life.

—Trinh Minh-ha, *When the Moon Waxes Red*

1

Word Games

"What's-his-name, the guy at William Morris, you know, who represents what's-his-face, the writer-director of *Field of Dreams*..."

"The baseball movie? All those dead players coming?"

We are by the pool, up on the roof of Le Bel Age Hotel, vistaing, waiting for a call. My lawyer and me. Los Angeles surrounds us, its margins seeking sanctuary in the spreading smog.

"That's the one," I say.

"What about him?"

"Who?"

"The agent. Peter Bandy."

"Yeah, that's his name. Peter-don't-call-me-Pete Bandy. Pass-the-pasta Pete. His assistant said he was operated on last week. They took out a foot and a half of his lower intestine. First-degree colitis, or something."

"Ouch."

"Shitty thing to happen," I say.

"You can say."

"So what do you think he's left with? What do you think?"

"I don't know," my lawyer says. "A bag or something?"

"A semicolon."

My lawyer laughs. I curl up the corner of my mouth, satisfied at my performance, the laconic, knowing delivery, and settle back into the chaise lounge.

"Yeah," I say. "Pretty funny."

"You kids," says my lawyer.

"I know," I say. "Not only that, I'm even younger than I look. Handsomer, too."

My lawyer chuckles and shakes his head. His gray beard moves in counterpoint to his face.

"I tell my wife," my lawyer says, "I say to her, my favorite clients, the ones I like best, are the ones with a sense of humor. I tell you, you don't have a sense of humor, this business'll kill you. It's one of the first rules."

"Rules of the game," I say.

"Of the game," he says.

My lawyer reaches down to his belt and sucks in his already girdled gut. With a deftness worthy of Clint Eastwood, he unsnaps the holster flap that secures his Motorola. He removes the phone and places it on the table between us, careful to keep its gunmetal gray plastic casing in the umbrella shade and out of the toxin-mediated sun.

"You think he'll call?"

"He'll call. It's his move. He knows it. He'll call."

"And if he doesn't?"

"Then what-the-hay," says my lawyer. "We'll call him one more time."

A cluster of toy soldiers sits on the radiator by the window through which I can see Freddie's pale yellow Rolls Royce basking in the late morning West Hollywood sun. The license plate does a little shimmer for me, FF4 dancing in the refracted light of an imperfect pane.

Freddie sits down awkwardly opposite us, positioning himself between me and the sunlit window so that his face is backlit, making any expression he might produce hard for me to read.

My lawyer sits next to me on the low black-and-white zebra-striped sofa. His beard covers the knot in his Hermès tie, his paunch the buckle of his Gucci belt. But his pants don't quite cover the top of his frayed and threadbare socks.

Freddie looks uncomfortable in his chair.

"Back problems," he says. "Excuse my discomfort."

"Lower back?" I ask.

"Ummm," he says.

"I had the operation," I say. "About six years ago. Partial disk removal. Avoid it at all costs."

"I have," he says. "So far. Thank you for the advice."

This is Freddie Fields, former president of MGM, former agency head, the man who made Steve McQueen, who produced *The Year of Living Dangerously*, *Looking for Mr. Goodbar*, and *Lipstick*, among others. Freddie, who looks just like Frank Sinatra minus the scowl, who is old now, but whose mind is said to be young. Freddie, still a major player, although he claims to be semiretired, cultivating the image of an occasional dabbler.

Watch out for Freddie, everybody always says. He'll pat you on the back with one hand and stab you in the gut with the other.

"You know what you've done with this script, don't you," says Freddie. "You've turned the cliche inside out. You've deconstructed the bank robber myth. It's a magnificent piece of work. It's a South African *Bonnie and Clyde* without the distraction of Bonnie, with the evils of apartheid taking the place of the Depression. You have my profound congratulations on a brilliant screenplay."

My lawyer clears his throat and sits up as straight as forward-rotating shoulders will permit.

"Glad you liked it, Freddie," he says. "I thought you would."

"Coffee?" asks Freddie. "A cool drink, some Perrier?"

"A Coke," I say, "would help."

"Coffee, black," says my lawyer.

Freddie presses a button on the phone next to him.

"Did you get that, angel?" he says.

A disembodied voice replies, "Yes, Mr. Fields."

Freddie smiles at me.

"Technology," he says.

"It's everywhere," I say. "You can't hide anymore..."

"So," he says, "Tell me about the rights."

"They rest," says my lawyer, "with my client's company, under renewable option for a period of three years. No liens, no encumbrances, no attachments, no complications. The chain of title is unimpeachable."

"That's very reassuring."

A fast-walking, tall girl with big hair, big lips, and a tiny waist strides through the door and places a tray on the table between us.

"Thank you, Glynis," says Freddie. "Glynis, this is Mr. Kohn and his attorney, Mr. Rosenberg."

Glynis smiles and says with an English accent, "Gentlemen," as she retires.

On the tray next to the coke and coffee is a glass of water. Freddie picks it up and uses it to wash down two pills that he takes from his shirt pocket.

"Doctors," he says.

"I know," I say.

"So tell me," says Freddie between capsules, "what can I do to help?"

"Well," I say, "we're looking to put a package together, including above-the-line financing. I think we can get some below-the-line money out of South Africa, if we shoot it there, which could prove a problem because of sanctions and all, but on the whole—"

"If we get the right people involved, financing's not a problem and we can shoot it anywhere. Anywhere that'll work for the story."

"South Africa," I say, "is right."

"But," says my lawyer, "there is always Zimbabwe or even Kenya—"

"Whatever," says Freddie. "Those are details. I am thinking . . . to direct, Peter Weir. And Mel Gibson to star."

"Well," I say.

"Yes," says my lawyer. "Now you're talking."

"Well," I say. "Yes."

Then I say, "We were kind of leaning toward Rutger Hauer. He looks exactly like the real bank robber looked—Andre Stander was a real person, you understand—and Hauer's Dutch so the accent would be right. I hear from William Morris that he's available and . . ."

Freddie watches me patiently, but I am not sure he's listening. I stop talking. I hear my voice trailing off; I hear it still saying things several seconds after I think I have stopped.

"You know," he says, "in this town, Mel Gibson is the hottest game going. Top box office draw. Instantly bankable. Rutger Hauer is, undeniably, a fine actor, and he is also a personal friend of mine. Rutger and I go way back. We have shared many things . . ."

Then Freddie's eyes lock onto me as he continues talking, not missing a beat, not altering tone or decibel level.

". . . but in this town, Rutger Hauer has cholera, Rutger Hauer is yesterday's donut, Rutger Hauer is a joke, Rutger Hauer's name is never mentioned in mixed company. In this town, Rutger Hauer is shit."

Over Freddie's shoulder I see an old black man start to rub the Rolls with a new chamois cloth. He looks like he is whistling, like he is happy in his work.

"Scratch," says my lawyer with a nervous laugh, "Rutger Hauer."

Freddie's eyes are still on me. It is hard to see into them, shaded as they are by that carefully constructed backlight. I think, even if I could see into them, I would find nothing recognizable, nothing with which I am remotely familiar.

"Do you really think Mel Gibson will do it?" I ask.

"I don't know," says Freddie. "But I can get him and Peter scripts. I know they want to work together again—and with me again. And how different can South Africa be from Indonesia? Not very, I venture to say."

"Well . . . " I say.

"So, I can talk to them," says Freddie, uninterested in anything I might have to say. As if I hadn't started to speak. "Would you like me to do that, to talk to them?"

"We haven't," says my lawyer to Freddie, "talked about your deal."

"I don't know," says Freddie. "At this stage of my life, I don't really care about things like that. I just want to help get good movies made, and I think this will make a damn good movie. I'm out of the money-power game now. I've done all that. I've got a few movies left in me, a little time, and I want to make sure that they're important films, that they say something that needs to be said."

"Executive producer credit?" asks my lawyer. "With my client producing."

"Whatever," says Freddie.

Freddie looks at me. This is suddenly his game, his rules. I don't know what else to do. I nod.

"Angel," he says, as if into the air, not to us, to no one present. His finger has already depressed the button.

"Yes, Mr. Fields," comes the reedy English voice, disembodied, plastic.

"If the hour's right and we're not going to wake him up, get me Peter in Sydney and then Mel. He's probably in London. Otherwise, get me Mel first."

"Right away, Mr. Fields."

I stand up and walk around Freddie to the window.

"And, angel," I hear Freddie say. "Confirm lunch with Armand Hammer at the Polo Lounge. Tell him I'll be about twenty minutes late. And get Sven Nyquist on hold. I'll talk to him from the car."

"Yes, Mr. Fields."

"What are the toy soldiers for?" I ask.

"I'm doing a film next summer down in the Carolinas. A Civil War piece about a Negro regiment. Right now it's called *Glory*. Matthew Broderick'll star. I got those little plastic guys because I wanted to get some idea of what a hundred soldiers looks like."

Sitting there on Freddie Fields's radiator, they don't look like much.

Hank Snow sings "There Goes My Everything" on the car radio.

"Hey," says my lawyer. "We anted up. We put the script on the table, Freddie put up his connections. The cards were dealt. Now we play our hand. Which ain't bad, I must say. You're batting in the big leagues now, kid. You're going to be a part of it all."

"Ante up," I say, "doesn't mean he sticks his butt in my face."

"He did that?" asks my lawyer. "Was I there? Did I miss something?"

"Rutger Hauer."

"Rutger Hauer?" says my lawyer. "Who the fuck cares about Rutger Hauer?"

*　　*　　*

"Don't ask me why Mel is doing *Hamlet*, don't ask me why Mel does anything. Mel is Mel. Too much kangaroo meat makes the brain go hippity hop, hippity hop."

It is Sabra talking, one of Freddie's right hands, an Israeli woman with a cigarette and blonde hair and graying roots.

"And Peter Weir?" I ask.

"Why would Peter do it without Mel?" Sabra says.

"Why, indeed," I say.

The office is small and cramped, across the hall from Freddie's. There is a single aloe plant next to the tiny window. We sit on low chairs across a glass-topped table littered with Diet Coke cans. My lawyer has long since taken the red-eye east.

"What's Freddie say?" I ask.

"Freddie," says Sabra.

I can hear his voice across the hall, talking to someone, the door open. A sudden crescendo.

"I don't give a fuck! Tell that asshole I don't give a fuck! Tell him it's my fucking movie, goddam it! My fucking money!" Freddie's voice.

Sabra gets up and shuts her door. As she does, I see Freddie's door slam shut. It closes without a bang, the sound more like a whump, that suction sound that a toilet plunger makes, the sound of soundproofing.

Sabra sits down and lights another Gauloise.

"Let me tell you," she says. "There are things . . ."

She doesn't finish the sentence. She looks at me for a long time.

Finally, she says, "But there is some good news."

"There is?"

"I have it out to three very fine directors, first class, A list, bankable directors that I think would be perfect for this film. Three at the same time. You know I'm not supposed to do that. You have to send it to only one at a time. Those are the rules. I break rules," she says.

"You do?"

"It's how I got where I am today."

She stubs out her half-smoked cigarette and flips her hair back.

"Rutger Hauer," she says, "came by the other day."

The pause is pregnant. She continues, assured that she has my attention.

"Freddie sent him the script. He read it and he flipped and he flipped out. Both, at the same time. He came in here on his motorcycle, some big Harley, rode it right up next to Freddie's Rolls. Revved it up and spit exhaust all over Freddie's fender. He was all in black leather and he had a can of beer in his hand and two more stuck in his pockets. Freddie and I talked to him. He drank, he paraded, he yelled, he acted. He wants the part, he'll kill for the part. He came fucking dressed for the part. It's so wonderful."

"But Freddie said that Rutger Hauer—"

"Rutger's an option, a chip we play," she says slowly, painfully, as if talking to a petulant child. "It doesn't mean he will end up in the picture. But with him, maybe we can get Phillip Noyce to direct. Universal is hot on Phillip now."

"Phillip who?"

"Noyce. From New Zealand or somewhere like that."

"What about the three directors? Who are they?"

"I can't say right now. You know that. If they find out . . . I will tell you as soon as I can. Promise."

"And Rutger Hauer?"

"I'm stringing him along. Actors love that. A phone call a day. A drink or two. Asking him what he thinks. Telling him how good he looks, how smart he is. Knowing what he wants to hear and then dangling it in front of him, just out of reach. You know, stringing him along."

"It all sounds," I say, "depressingly familiar."

"Whatever," says Sabra. " I thought you'd be happy about Rutger. Listen, be happy, okay?"

"Do I have a choice?"

"Yes, you do. You can be unhappy. But I'd be happier if you were happy. So, make me happy. Be happy, too."

"Let you string me along?"

"Hey," she says, "it's better than a poke in the eye with a hot stick."

I am eating a poached egg on toast. The toast is warm and buttered, the egg firm on the outside, liquid in the inside—everything is just right.

"I love this place," says my lawyer, now back from Boston. "I always stay here. How do you like the food?"

"Taste's like shit," I say. "Taste's like show biz."

"That good, huh?"

We are having breakfast in the guests-only restaurant somewhere near the top of L'Ermitage Hotel in Beverly Hills. We are waiting for Ari to arrive.

"How do I get myself into these things?" I say. "How do things get to where they get, always where I don't want them to be? How?"

"You're not changing your mind again, are you?" asks my lawyer. "The man is bringing a check. You realize that. A check."

"Fucking Freddie," I say. "No Mel, no Peter, no Rutger, no Phillip Noyce, no Universal, no anybody, just Sabra talking and talking, and Freddie, he stopped taking my calls weeks ago. And now Ari, some Greek who makes exploitation pictures, for God's sake."

"I sat with Freddie yesterday," says my lawyer. His patience is measured, a lawyerly tone, as if to a murderer about to be sentenced. "We went down the list. He spoke to six major studios, three mini-majors, ten A-list actors, and who knows how many directors. They all passed. Nobody wants to do it. Do you understand that?"

"Maybe," I say, "they passed because of Freddie."

"Get real," says my lawyer.

"How real do you want me to get?" I say.

"I know Ari," he says. "Ari gets pictures made. They might not be the greatest things on celluloid, but he gets them made and they make money. Ari is doing this as a personal favor to Freddie. Ari owes Freddie a favor. Freddie introduced him to the girl he married."

"Jesus Christ," I say, "what the fuck!"

"Ari is bringing a check for forty-five thousand dollars. That money will be divided among you, the writer guy, and me. I've got a fortune in this thing in hard cash, not to mention billable hours. So do you. Let's cut our losses and let Ari expose himself for a while."

"Fuck Ari."

"Get real, goddam it!"

I don't say anything.

"Then what the hell are we doing here?" he says.

He moves the bacon around on his plate. Then he speaks in a calmed voice.

"Look, Ari has it for three years. If nothing happens, it reverts to you and he's out forty-five thousand dollars plus. We've got nothing to lose and—"

A tall thin man in a silk suit enters the restaurant. My lawyer stands up and smiles as Ari approaches. Under his breath and between his teeth, my lawyer says to me, "Just sign the goddam agreements."

Then he says, "Ari!"

They embrace, all smiles and backslapping bonhomie.

"I have wonderful news, gentlemen," says Ari, talking as much with his arms as with his mouth. "Jon Voight loves the script. He will make a brilliant Stander!"

We drink coffee and exchange pleasantries. Ari eats half a melon.

"You have a wonderful project," he says. "I congratulate you."

I say nothing. I wonder how much the rings on his fingers cost.

"I promise you," he says, "a quality film. It will be my passion."

"That's good," I hear myself saying. "Passion is always good."

Out of his fat black briefcase, my lawyer produces four copies of a professionally bound-in-blue legal agreement. We all read it. We all sign each of the four copies.

From his inside jacket pocket, Ari pulls out a single, somewhat wrinkled blank check. It is from Barclay's Bank, London. With a Mount Blanc pen, Ari writes it out in favor of us in the amount of forty-five thousand dollars and signs it with a Mediterranean flourish.

"We have," says my lawyer, "memorialized this moment."

We shake hands, a round robin of pressed flesh. And then suddenly it's over. My lawyer and Ari leave; they have other matters to discuss elsewhere. I linger over my grapefruit, alone at the table.

My lawyer deposits the check in a Boston bank the next day. It bounces. He has to deposit it two more times before it clears.

Ari never makes the movie.

On the phone. Nine months later.

"Hello, Sabra?" I say.

"Yes?"

"This is Nate Kohn."

A long pause.

"Nate Kohn?" says Sabra. "Do I know you?"

Autobiographical sketches offer another example of ways of breaking with the chain of invisibility. Diaries, memoirs, and recollections are widely used by marginalized people to gain a voice and to enter into the area of visibility. As strategies . . . they retain all their subverting potential. For with the displacement effected on the opposition between the private and the public—prominent in the critical works of peoples of color as well as of the women's movements—autobiographical forms do not necessarily implicate narcissism, and the personal becoming communal no longer functions as mere privileged access to the private realm of an individual. Memories within come out of the material that precedes and defines a person. When she creates, they are the subsoil of her work. Thus, autobiography both as singularity and as collectivity is a way of making history and rewriting culture.

—Trinh Minh-ha, *When the Moon Waxes Red*

No duality is inferred by the Two, no uniformity implied in the One, but above all, no compromise meant by "middle." Rather, what is involved is a state of alert in-betweenness and "critical" non-knowingness, in which the bringing of reflective and cosmic memory to *life*—that is, to the *formlessness of form*—is infinitely more exigent than the attempt to "express," to judge or evaluate.

—Trinh Minh-ha, *When the Moon Waxes Red*

The real world appears in the image as [if] it were between parentheses.

—Homi Bhabha, *The Location of Culture*

2

The Ticket

"You know the monorail at the New York World's Fair?" Harry says. "John bought it. When was it, John? 1962? '64?"

"'62 or '64."

John's Texas-sized body fills a large wingback chair. John's wife Shana sits in its mate. Between them is a mahogany table with two Tiffany lamps on it.

"What'd you do with it?" Harry says. Harry is the writer.

"I guess I still have it. In a warehouse down near Brownsville somewhere."

Shana smiles graciously. She is pale. She wears a red Hermès scarf wrapped turban-like around her head.

"You're something, John," says Harry. "You really are. Tell him about the carpet, John. I love the one about the carpet."

"It used to belong to the Shah," John says.

"John hired some guys to go in and get it during the revolution. Took it right out of the palace in Teheran."

The carpet is large, thick, intricate, beautiful. About the size of a basketball court. I hadn't noticed it before. It doesn't quite fill the room.

"Do you know Burt?" John asks.

I say no.

"I could have gotten him to help a couple of years ago. After the Cannonball movies, before he did that thing with Dolly Parton."

"*Whorehouse*," Harry says.

I sit on one end of a long white sofa. Harry sits in the middle, about ten feet from me. You could play shuffleboard on that sofa.

"How about Bob?" asks John. "Bob Redford."

I say I met him once, briefly. He is shorter than he looks, I say. And then I tell John about my Lebanese friend Anis, who is now a big-time Italian producer, and how his first job in the business was digging holes in hard Greek ground for Sophia Loren to stand in. So she wouldn't tower over Alan Ladd when they kissed. I want to mention the name of the film, but I can't remember it.

Shana smiles. Nobody else does. The story normally gets a laugh.

"Have you asked this Anis for the money?"

I explain that producers never have money. Producers get money from other people. I know. I am a producer. But, yes, I say, I asked Anis.

"Damn," says John. "Seven years ago I could have just written you a check. Now . . . now, they have me all tied up."

"You still have the house," says Harry.

"And a few of the cars," says John. "You saw the Testarossa out front. And the two Rolls."

"John loves his cars," says Shana.

"And the artwork," says Harry. "The Remington is still in the gun room."

I count the Tiffany lamps. There are twenty-seven of them.

"I could call Jim Nabors in Hawaii," says John.

"He'd want to be in it," says Harry.

"I know," says John.

Nobody says anything for a while. Things aren't going well.

"What about the guys in Arkansas?" says John. "Do you know Win? I could call Win."

I say Rockefellers don't invest in movies. They support the arts with charitable donations. I met Win, was introduced to him once, I say, but on the unspoken condition I never ask for cash. The Rockefellers are like royalty in this country.

"Movie stars are the real royalty," says Harry. "They're who people really want to hobnob with. Hell, they're the people the Rockefellers want to hobnob with."

I say I guess so.

"And Don Tyson? The chicken farmer?" says John. "He owns every chicken west of the Mississippi, and most of them east of the river, too. A real peckerwood, that one. I met him in the West Indies once. Drunk as a skunk. Neck redder than Shana's scarf."

"Snopes," says Harry. "One of the Snopeses."

I tell Harry how good he is at finding literary references, that it is an underappreciated talent. Then I mention that I read about Tyson giving Willie Nelson money to make a Western a few years ago. The picture died. Once burned . . .

"Willie Nelson," says John. "Jesus Christ."

"Peckerwood," says Harry.

"You need two million," says John.

I say we could do it with one-eight, maybe.

"Two," says Harry. "We really need two."

Always worried about his salary, Harry. Always thinking that it will be his fees that will be cut first.

"I have an idea," says John. "Maybe I can help after all."

John stands up. He is tall, well over six foot, big but not fat. Thick mane of graying hair. Alligator boots and a hand-hammered silver belt buckle.

"Be right back . . ." he says.

Shana smiles. She waits until he's left the room.

"John's changed, don't you think, Harry?"

"I don't know," says Harry. "John's John."

"After he had to sell the Saints and the banks took the hotels and he lost most of the oil wells . . . After that, well, he did change."

She looks over at me.

"You know his daddy built the fortune up from nothing, an oil empire, stretching clear from Galveston to Lake Charles. Thank God he didn't live to see what happened. After the crash, after the banks and the lawyers carved everything up, John sat in that chair for three months. Day after day, staring off into space. Thinking mostly about his daddy, he said . . ."

She raises her hand to her face, a finger gently stroking her cheek.

"He's changed, all right," she says to Harry. "All this trouble has changed him. He had to give up the Indy racing team, too. Did you know that, Harry?"

"I heard," says Harry. "Damn shame."

"He loved it so," says Shana.

She shifts slightly, painfully in her chair. I can see her left temple now. There is no hair there. Then I remember that Harry said something about chemotherapy.

"This movie business would cheer him up, I think," she says. "A way back for him. He loves being around movie people . . ."

John returns with a small wooden box. He opens it and spills the contents onto the coffee table.

"Gold coins," says John. "Remember that Portuguese galleon I found off the Florida coast? Near as I can figure, it went down about 1590. I did some of the diving myself. I was younger, then."

"That's right," says Harry. "With Peter Blatty or somebody."

A couple of the coins roll onto the floor.

"See what you can get for 'em," says John. "If you can sell 'em for a million, I'll put the money into the movie. Nobody'll know, except us. These aren't listed assets, if you understand what I'm saying."

I finger the coins. They are heavy. Some are in little glassine envelopes, others are not. I pick up the ones from the floor. Some are pristine, others are so worn the images are barely visible. I count them out. There are forty-eight of them, most small, but some the size of silver dollars.

"And if I'm in, I can guarantee Don Tyson will come in, too. Let me tell you something. There's nothing new money likes better than being in bed with old money."

I say thank you.

"If you set it up," says John, "I'll take the meeting with Tyson. I'll do that for you."

"I'm excited," says Harry. He smiles at John. "You're going to get that executive producer credit for sure, John!"

"Whatever's comfortable for you boys," says John.

"We'll premiere the fucker at Cannes," says Harry. "Pardon my French, Shana."

Shana smiles at Harry.

"The South of France in May," says John. "White asparagus on the Eden Roc terrace. You'd like that, wouldn't you, Shana?"

"Yes, John," she says. "That would be really fine."

The coins are heavy, the thought of turning them into greenbacks even heavier. I still don't know how I am going to pay the actors and crew on Friday.

"You like the office?"

We are standing next to the French doors that open onto the rose garden. Only there isn't a rose garden. Just a parking lot baking in the hot Arkansas sun.

"I'm real proud of this office."

John towers over all of us, particularly Don, who is short and pudgy in his starched light brown overalls. "Don" is stitched in red over his heart. "Tyson Foods" more than covers his back, the T folded up in his left armpit.

"Please, sit."

Tod sits next to me, John in the black lacquered chair on one side of the doors. Don in the other.

"I did some work for Jimmy Carter when he was president," says Don. "Headed up a commission on agriculture. Anyhow, I walk into the oval office the first time and I say to myself holy shit. I fall in love with the fucking place. So when we built the new headquarters here, I had 'em make my office exactly like the oval office. That desk there is a duplicate of Jimmy's desk. The flags Jimmy gave me. I only changed one thing. I made it bigger. One point five times scale. Don't know how Jimmy could work in that goddam shoe box."

"The Oval Office right here in Arkansas," says Tod. "I never would have imagined. And I drive by here near every day."

Don's eyes are glassy and red. His skin is puffy and bad. But his face shines, as if it has been waxed and highly polished.

"We've met before, I'm sure," says John. "Was it on St. Barts?"

"Bimini," says Don. "You had a drink on my boat. Bum Phillips was there. I was with Julia, a former Miss Tennessee. Jugs like cantaloupes. You only stayed a couple of minutes."

"A magnificent boat," says John. He smiles a winning smile.

"Sixty-five foot. Take a girl down there, she turns into a wild animal. Something about boats."

Tod clears his throat and says, "It's good of you to see us on such short notice." Tod wipes his palms on his pants. Tod has

$250,000 in the movie. We spent the last of it a couple of days ago.

"Hey," says Don. "Anything to oblige."

"Don," says John, "Let's talk about the movie."

"Lemme say right off the bat, John," says Don, "lemme tell you, I know fuck-all about movies."

"These boys have done a magnificent job putting this thing together," says John. "It's a great story, set here in the Ozarks. They've assembled a first-rate cast. Hal Holbrook's directing. You know, Mark Twain."

"Don't know squat about actors," says Don. "'Cept Willie, who can't act for shit. But, go on."

"The bottom line," says John, "is that they had some bad luck. The investors fell out at the last minute. Hell, it can happen to anybody. They've been working here for five weeks, put it all together on next to nothing, and are supposed to start shooting on Monday. Woody, the bartender from *Cheers*, he's in it."

"I think I saw something on the TV," says Don.

"I'm putting in a million, Don," says John. "I'd like you to match that."

Don smiles.

"Hell," says John, "they might even give you a part in it."

"Now that would be something," says Don.

We wait. Tod rubs his hands together and wipes them on his pants again.

"Like I said earlier, I don't know nothing about movies," says Don. "Hell, I don't even go see 'em in the theater. Well, take that back. If there's some girl I want to fuck and she really wants to see a movie bad, then maybe I'll go. I saw *Dirty Dancing* that way. I thought it was a piece of shit, but then what do I know. At least I got laid."

"It's shooting right here in your own backyard, Don," says John. "In Northwest Arkansas."

"And it's good for Northwest Arkansas," says Tod. "It'll show us up right."

I try to look earnest, to will it, to will the right words out of his mouth.

"I got a rule about business," says Don. "I never put money into anything I know fuck-all about."

John looks at Don for what seems like a long time. He then carefully puts his fingertips together and raises his thumbs to his chin. He smiles at Don, a gloriously generous smile.

"Well," says John, "are you planning to go down to your boat any time soon, Don? Weather's perfect this time of year."

We are walking fast down the hallway, away from the Oval Office. John, Tod, and me.

"I thought when he said he'd meet you—" says Tod.

"It was about something else," says John. "It wasn't about the movie at all."

"I'm real sorry about this," says Tod, "Sorry to bring you all this way . . ."

"What about the coins?" says John.

I say that Sotheby's has appraised them for $350,000, and an outfit in Las Vegas thinks they can get $375,000 for them, but it'd take a month.

"That's a far cry from a million," says John. "It really has to be a million. They're worth way more than that, fellows."

I say that time is running out.

"I don't know what else I can do," says John.

Neither do I, I say.

We have reached the car. I don't remember leaving the building.

"We have an hour before my plane," says John. "Any chance I could meet Hal Holbrook?"

The production office is in an abandoned Chrysler dealership across from the Hilton in downtown Fayetteville. The entire cast and crew is gathered in the new car showroom. A horseshoe of forty unsmiling faces stares at me. Holbrook is perched on a stool off to the side. John is back in Houston. Tod is at his house in Rogers. Nobody knows where Harry is.

A lot of them, mostly the locals, carry cameras. They know, of course.

I try to project my voice, to give it weight, as I tell them that we've run out of money, that I am shutting the picture down. The return portions of their air tickets are still good, I say. Then I tell them that there is no money to pay this week's salaries. I say I am sorry, I don't know what else to say.

"These things happen," says Holbrook. "It's nobody's fault. With the best of intentions, these things sometimes happen. This isn't the first time for me, although I hope to God it's the last."

A few smiles. Holbrook is still talking.

"If you want to be in this business, you have to understand that sometimes pictures collapse. It's a risky business, fed by dreams. Dreams are not always the strongest foundation."

Holbrook is standing now.

"Anybody want to say anything?"

Woody says, "Yeah, well, shit."

The cameraman says to me, "You know you'll be hearing from my lawyer."

"And my agent," says Bonnie.

"What about . . ." says David, a New York actor who is playing the lead. He stands up—actors always stand to talk. "What about if we took less, deferred our salaries, or something. I mean, hell, we're already here."

I say that wouldn't work. I say we are heavily in debt with no prospects for investment whatsoever. We can't pay the hotel bill or buy film stock. I thank him. I say we'll try to get it together again, maybe next spring. And if we do, we want everybody to come back. I tell them how wonderful they are.

"Look at all these people," says Woody. "Some of them, they quit real jobs to do this. What the hell you going to do about them?"

A production secretary from Fayetteville says, "This was my chance, my chance to make it, and it's gone now."

She starts to cry. She looks at me, really mad now, and yells through her tears, "You robbed me, you robbed me of my one chance! How dare you!"

"Damn right," says an older man, an actor from the Rep in Little Rock. "This was gonna be my ticket. You held out the carrot and now you take it away. You just can't do this to us, you can't!"

"Hey," says Woody, "this is some heavy shit you're dumping on us, man. You're responsible for a lot of people's lives here."

I don't say anything.

Holbrook puts his arm around the production secretary who is sobbing now, uncontrollably.

"Hey, darling," he says. "Come on, it's only a movie, a few weeks' work. It's not that bad."

But it is. It certainly is.

I look down from the hotel room window onto what once was the used car lot. Woody is gone, already on a plane. So is Bonnie. Hal and David are there, along with most of the local crew and cast. People are embracing and exchanging telephone numbers. Many of them are crying and most are drinking beer, as they take turns photographing each other with the Hollywood star and the New York actor. Pictures to remember this time, to capture that precious moment when they were a part of it all.

I pull the curtains and turn on the TV. For the next five or six hours I stare at the set. There is nothing else left to do.

I watch the movie grosses on *Entertainment Tonight* and a terribly earnest spokesmodel tell Ed about her dreams on *Star Search*. On *Lifestyles of the Rich and Famous*, I watch a bare-chested Robin Leach sun himself on the beach outside Larry Hagman's Malibu home. Larry wears a turban. And I see Johnny Carson play stump the band with a woman from Greenville, Mississippi, and a young man with a Wharton School MBA who says he wants to be a comedy writer.

About midnight, the phone rings.

"Asshole," a voice says. "We know where you live, you asshole."

I pull the jack out of the wall.

My wife says, "Maybe you should think about another line of work."

"I can't," I say. "I just can't, even if I wanted to."

PART II

OBSESSION

What is startling is the rapidity with which it has now become a commonplace that, precisely, any substance, any behavior, even any affect may be pathologized as addictive. Addiction, under this definition, resides only in the *structure* of a will that is always somehow insufficiently free, a choice whose volition is unsufficiently pure.

—Eve Kosofsky Sedgwick, "Epidemics of the Will"

Like the war weapon launched at full speed at the visual target it's supposed to wipe out, the aim of cinema will be to provoke an effect of vertigo in the voyeur-traveller; the end being sought now is to give him the impression of being projected into the image.

—Paul Virilio, *The Aesthetics of Disappearance*

3

Oh, Dear, What Can the Matter Be?

Lament

Oh, dear, what can the matter be?
Oh, dear, what can the matter be?
Oh, dear, what can the matter be?
Johnny's so long at the fair.

(*The Real Mother Goose* 1916, p. 127)

Imagine the melody, a lone thin voice, questioning, worrying, trying to sing away the desperation. Another soul lost to Show Biz. The culture industry. Johnny seduced, co-opted, captured, displayed. In the end, when others invade his space and steal his voice, then what of poor Johnny? No doubt then a ruin of a boy, reduced, without even the crutch of melancholy, to barking for his supper.

The fair? Nothing's fair.

Cabaret

A diminutive bird of a woman, hair bobbed, Louised as someone once said, rewrites Cole Porter as she sings, working Reagan and

Bush into the lyric, politicking to the converted, making them laugh at a thousand points of light and other present foibles (this time to the Porter melody "Let's Do It, Let's Fall in Love"):

> Tired sluts from old Winnipeg do it
> Pit bulls having luncheon on your leg do it
> Most any red-blooded male does it
> When he gets a bit tight
> Vice President Quayle does it
> But it never seems right
> The Reagans, Nancy and Ron, do it
> Probably will live to see their son do it
> Let's do it
> Let's fall in love[1]

Sharon is her name. Cole Porter is her God, Gershwin her passion, Edith her idol.

Afterward, I speak to her, a shower of faded rose petals settled about her dainty feet, the two of us alone amid the rubble of an opening- (and closing-) night celebration, a Little Rock night, when Clinton was still governor and anything was possible.

"You should," I say, "bill yourself as the Great American Piaf."

"You want me to be," she asks, "an event?"

Epidemic

> Or, starving acrobat, you display for sale
> Your charms and smile, soaked with unseen tears,
> To cheer the spleen of the vulgar herd.
>
> (Baudelaire 1962, p. 16)

Some say the stage is a calling, like the ministry or the sea. Others say that it is an obsession, an addiction, a disease. For me, as I look around in that time and place, it's an epidemic. The Hollywood flu, and I'm infecting everyone I meet, despite the horror of that automobile showroom in Fayetteville only a few short weeks before.

Sharon is one of many caught up in the rush. Our paths cross in the social swirl of Little Rock where, for over ten years, she has made her living performing at weddings, business receptions, the local repertory theater, doing commercial voice-overs, and writing and producing the occasional one-woman show. Everything she does is enthusiastically received and reviewed, a star in her own place, a classic big-fish-in-a-small-pond success. But she reads Dorothy Parker and Truman Capote and dreams of New York. An eccentric Southern woman who finds few kindred souls at home, she seeks guidance from palmists, companionship with spirit guides, the future in Tarot cards. Her wish images are a succession of specific visions, ranging from seeing herself as a regular on *Saturday Night Live* to watching herself perform a one-woman show at Carnegie Hall. For a time, she looks to me as a channel into that dream world.

> I'm reserved about Harry
> And he's reserved about me
> No aggravations, expectations
> Projections of fantasy
> I take my lithium daily
> And he's in group therapy
> Oh, I'm reserved about Harry
> And he's reserved about—
> I've just filed against Harry
> Before he filed against me
> We can't afford it
> But we're so bored it
> Beats watching TV
> Oh why oh why did I marry
> And bury my identity?
> If only I'd been more wary—
> Now there's no pack of lies
> He can't analyze
> He's transformed himself
> I am on the shelf
> I'm not well without
> I'm in hell without
> There is not a doubt
> He is fine without . . . Me.[2]

Basking

> The theater's "games" and "plays" (until the end of the six-
> teenth century the words were interchangeable) were perceived
> by many of the "better sort" as pagan entertainments indistin-
> guishable from fairs, where the godly would only find "sinfull,
> heathenish, lewde, ungodly Spectacles, and most pernicious
> Corruptions." (Stallybrass and White 1986, p. 65)

Stallybrass and White's investigation of English and European
sixteenth- through eighteenth-century fairs, where Johnny innocently ventured to buy a bunch of blue ribbons, reveals them to
be as much theater as marketplace, a site of performance where

> [S]oothsayers and clairvoyants would usurp the prophetic roles
> of the preacher; actors would, literally, make a mummery of
> historical heroes and contemporary pretension, quacks and al-
> chemists would take the place of physicians, and peddlers and
> hawkers that of guildsmen. Its stables were dwellings for those
> who had no fixed abode, no claims on "burgerschap" (residen-
> tial citizenship); gypsies, transient musicians, and tumblers; ex-
> otics of doubtful origin; freed slaves with hair-raising tales of
> Turkish barbarity; and the ultimate parody of the "normal"—
> freaks, midgets, and giants. (Stallybrass and White 1986)

Stallybrass and White unpack Bakhtin's vision of fairs and
carnivals—places of inversion and hybridization, where anything
is possible and dreams come true, "a world of topsy-turvy, of
heteroglot exuberance, of ceaseless overrunning and excess where
all is mixed, hybrid, ritually degraded and defiled" (Stallybrass
and White 1986, p. 8).

This seemingly archaic site, the carnival (or fair), has suddenly, as Stallybrass and White point out, become "a mode of
understanding, a positivity, a cultural analytic.... Everywhere in
literary and cultural studies today we see carnival emerging as
a model, as an ideal..." (Stallybrass and White 1986, p. 6). Even
Foucault has his new historian, the genealogist,

> [K]now[ing] what to make of this masquerade. He will not
> be too serious to enjoy it; on the contrary, he will push the

> masquerade to its limits and prepare the great carnival of time
> where masks are constantly reappearing. Genealogy is history
> in the form of a concerted carnival. (Foucault 1977, pp. 160–61)

A seductive metaphor for contemporary times, the fair (or carnival) is a vivid site of performance where those who seek a stage and an audience come together to act out their dreams, their hopes, their very lives. I am not talking here so much about the limp remnants of carnival—the traveling circuses that perform at county fairgrounds under Rotary Club sponsorship, the farmer's markets, the weekend fairs at shopping malls, not even New Orleans's Mardi Gras or Rio's Carnival.[3]

I am talking about the great affective machine that today maps our very existence, that amorphous yet omnipresent site where everything is possible and nothing is forbidden, where exhibitionism and voyeurism combine in exaltation, where glory and fame are the promised pleasures, where the spotlight always shines and basking in its glow is synonymous with orgasm. I am talking about the entertainment/information regime, the culture industry, about Hollywood in all its spreading incarnations.

Confession

> Disgust always bears the imprint of desire. These low domains,
> apparently expelled as "Other," return as the object of nostalgia, longing and fascination. The forest, the fair, the theatre,
> the slum, the circus, the sea-side resort, the "savage": all these,
> placed at the outer limit of civil life, become symbolic contents
> of bourgeois desire. (Stallybrass and White 1986, p. 191)

In that Arkansas place, I call myself a movie producer. I am living there at the urging of an investment banker who employs me to run a regional feature film production development/finance company. I am doing this after several difficult years in Hollywood, the plan being to storm the gates with independent films made elsewhere, rather than bang my head against the walls built by Freddie Fields and others of his ilk.

Sharon appeals to me as both performer and writer, and I ask her to write a screenplay, which she agrees to do after great hesitation and only after I say I will write it with her. Her hesitation comes, she says, because she has never written anything longer than a three-minute song.

The idea for the screenplay is mine, an odd germ that I think suits Sharon's sense of the surreal. That she might be (or become) repulsed by the idea, that she will probably (eventually) feel uncomfortable with its grotesqueness, that she might think (find) the whole enterprise beneath her,[4] never occurs to me. And if these things dance through her mind, she never lets on until much later, if at all. Effectively, the chance to get into movies—the film is also to feature her in a prominent role—is all that matters, and she leaps at the chance. It is, she says, her ticket out of Little Rock and onto the world's stage.

> Note that the figures of the collector, the ragpicker, and the detective wander through the fields of fossil and ruin, while the fields of action of the prostitute, the gambler, and the flaneur are those of wish images, and of the fetish as their phantasmagoric form.[5] (Buck-Morss 1989)

Not yet informed by Benjamin and Bakhtin, I confuse the sophistication of German cabaret with the baseness of carnival, cavalierly lumping the complex aesthetics of middle Europe into a bubbling middle-American cauldron that I stir with glee, a distraction I embrace after the disgrace of Fayetteville. I happily, innocently mix oil and water.

Novelty

On the video screen a succession of snowy images, badly edited together with the aid of two VCRs in Chuck Harris's Hancock Park living room:

```
A Japanese variety show host shouts and cackles
in his native tongue as a bound and gagged man
climbs into a front-loading washing machine. A
pretty girl presses wash, and he spins around and
around in soap suds. Seconds later, the machine is
```

stopped and the man jumps out, his chains undone, his mouth smiling. Applause.

CUT TO:

A black man impersonates the Jackson Five with the aid of four life-size puppets that dance on horizontal poles that extend from his body and magically follow his every gyration. He and the puppets lip-sync the song.

CUT TO:

A juggler plays "Flight of the Bumble Bee" by bouncing three balls on an over-sized electronic keyboard at his feet on the floor.

CUT TO:

Two men wearing only black bicycle shorts, geeky eyeglasses, tiny bow ties, and Oxford shoes sit side by side on a stage frantically slapping their bare bodies to produce a music of crescendoing rhythms that ends in a violent fist fight between these two supposedly classical musicians.

CUT TO:

A sword swallower sticks eight swords in his mouth, then rotates them.

CUT TO:

A man blows up a balloon to six feet in diameter and slowly climbs inside it. Then he pops his head out of the hole and does a bouncy dance around the stage to the blasting sound of "Rock 'n' Roll Music."

CUT TO:

Three men dressed as midget coal miners—their heads and arms are real, but their bodies are hidden in the coal bags they drag behind them, allowing them to manipulate fake truncated legs in a humorous manner—dance and lip-sync to Tennessee Ernie Ford singing "Sixteen Tons."

CUT TO:

A man swallows a cigarette lighter, then regurgitates it. Then he inhales lighter gas, then smoke from a cigarette, then soap. He exhales a large soap bubble filled with gas that explodes in flames when he ignites it with the lighter.

CUT TO:

A man does an impersonation of "split pea soup coming to a slow boil."

CUT TO:

A ventriloquist in a complicated suit changes places with his dummy: The man standing is a dummy, the head on the puppet is real. They sing opera.

CUT TO:

A man pops four ping-pong balls into his mouth.

CUT TO:

A woman plays common household items as musical instruments, including flower pots, pots and pans, a faucet (New Orleans jazz), a chair (a Sousa march), a toilet seat strung with harp strings.

CUT TO:

A man swallows swords, eats fire, chews on a string of razor blades. His piece de resistance consists of sucking dental floss up his nose, pulling it out his mouth and flossing his nose and throat.

CUT TO:

A man/woman sings a duet with him-/herself. One profile is Lionel Richie, the other is Diana Ross. He/she turns a lot, and duets "Touch Me in the Morning."

These are variety performers, some of Chuck Harris's clients. I've known Chuck for many years, watched him morph from a red-haired stand-up comic into a silver-haired Swifty Lazar clone, complete with oversized glasses, the image always degraded by a large Filipino cigar that he passes off as pure Havana. Mostly, his clients are very funny and watchable, the cream of the crop. They are contemporary nomads, calling a suitcase home, as they make a living working nightclubs, half-time shows at sporting events, and TV variety programs, mostly in Europe, South America, and Asia.

My idea is to weave these particular artists into the plot of a feature film. I see Sharon as one of them, a kindred spirit. And perhaps, by extension, I am one of them too, a wanderer prowling the murky waters just beyond the farthest reaches of the Hollywood tentacle. I call the project *East of the 7-11*, the title locating a mystical and mysterious utopia where variety performers share idyllic lives and perform for each other without complication or competition—until an outsider discovers them and seeks to exploit their bizarre talents.

The idea proves easier than the process.

Repetition

These variety performers are easy exemplars; they embody the obsession—the rush to become part of the culture industry. Whether their particular skill results from natural accident (e.g., double-jointedness) or years of painful practice (e.g., fire eating), they possess a valuable piece of cultural capital, one they can use to gain a place in the paying public's eye. Like Sharon, like me— like most everybody—they have felt the hegemonic shove toward the spotlight—toward the sense of liberation, self-realization, and ecstasy promised by the postmodern incarnation of the fair.

> All moveables of wonder from all parts
> Are here, Albinos, painted Indians, Dwarfs,
> The Horse of Knowledge, and the Learned Pig,
> The Stone-eater, the Man that swallows fire,

Giants, Ventriloquists, the Invisible Girl,
The Bust that speaks, and moves its goggling eyes,
The wax-work, Clock-work, all the marvellous craft
Of modern Merlins, wild Beasts, Puppet-shows,
All out-o'-th'way, far-fetch'd perverted things.
All freaks of Nature, all Promethean thoughts
Of Man; his dulness, madness, and their feats,
All jumbled together to make up
This Parliament of Monsters.

(Wordsworth 1959, ll. 686–94)

The skills of these modern-day monsters are honed, polished, and enhanced. What results is an act, a bit of business in which the performer specializes, an infinitely repeatable production that normally runs for about three minutes. But if it is good, it can keep you working for a lifetime. Look at Señor Wences, the Spanish ventriloquist who has spent half a century talking to a face drawn on his thumb and index finger. "Zaw right?" "Zaw right."

Condemned to the hell of continual repetition, night after night of the same song, the same dance, the same laughs, the same oohs and aahs in the same places, these performers nevertheless manage to approach each show afresh, as if Steven Spielberg—or a new lover—is always in the front row.

It is the manager's dilemma always to find new places for these acts to play, only one of many frustrations that plague his job. From the perspective of such a manager (Walter Benjamin might have called it a pimp's perspective), hell is something different, more profound. He always has to find new acts that, in fact, are merely more of the same, slight variations on the general theme of novelty. A chronic quest for more of the same, only different. His hell

> deals not with the fact that "always the same thing" happens (*a forteriori* this is not about eternal recurrence) but the fact that on the face of that oversized head called earth precisely what is newest doesn't change; that this "newest" in all its pieces keeps remaining the same. It constitutes the eternity of Hell and its sadistic craving for innovation. To determine the totality of features in which this "modernity" imprints itself would mean to represent Hell. (Benjamin 1999, pp. 842–43)

But for Chuck Harris, who followed his father into bur-
lesque as a top banana (the comedian who entertains between
the striptease acts) and who went on to play a supporting role on
Ozzie and Harriet and to become a mediocre stand-up comedian
before finding his gift in management, this hell is his heaven.

Every minute of his waking day—he sleeps four hours a
night—is spent finding and selling acts, arguing with bookers
and producers, traveling with his clients, and looking after their
money and by extension his commission. And then doing it all
over and over again, day and night, year after year. His heaven is
his total submersion in this industry to which he has miraculously
gained access—a heaven that he also relives and reconstructs in
the many stories his adventures allow him to tell to all who will listen, tales of the swell life starring that intrepid deal maker, Chuck.

For him, his discoveries are a phalanx of infinitely renewable
variety performers, a wedge that he drives before him into the
world. They are sources of irritation and delight, but foremost
they are talents that give him shape and purpose, a reservoir of
cultural capital that defines his being and guarantees his place in
the coveted spotlight. And any frustration or disdain he might
have, he reserves for the acts.

"Fuck 'em," says Chuck. "They need me a lot more than I
need them. Fuck the bastards. Fuck 'em if they can't take a joke."

"They'll do the movie, then," I say.

"Fuckin' A, they'll do the movie," says Chuck. "How's the
script coming?"

Creation

> There was an old maid from Chaillot
> Who lived upon frogs' tales and snot
> When she tired of these
> She consumed the green cheese
> That she scraped from the sides of her twat
>
> (Anonymous)

Sharon throws herself into the script, seeking out limericks for
a character she creates who speaks only in rhymes. She designs
another part for Joan, an actress friend of hers from San Diego who

once played Blanche in an award-winning repertory production of *A Streetcar Named Desire*. Sharon wants her to play Buttsky, a character that Joan does in her night club act. Joan, who can contort her body into a variety of outlandish positions, becomes Buttsky by donning a black leotard and lying upside down on her shoulders in a basket with her butt sticking up in the air. She puts a mouth and eyes on it and suddenly she is Buttsky. Buttsky tells butt jokes for twelve minutes. He does the same in our screenplay.

```
                    BUTTSKY
     Why do Mexicans eat beans every day? So
     they can take a bubble bath at night.

     What's soft and brown and sits on a
     piano bench? Beethoven's first movement.
```

Sharon of Cabaret is discovering that there is a seductive flip side to almost everything, and she is enjoying the vulgarity of the underbelly. Through Buttsky, Sharon proclaims, "Assholes of the world unite!"

I explain to her that we are working in a number of genres to generate a unique work. Our script is rooted in the late 1970s low-humor films like John Belushi's *National Lampoon's Animal House*. But we can also find traces from Joseph von Sternberg's *The Blue Angel* and Todd Browning's *Freaks* working their way into our screenplay. But Sharon doesn't care about antecedents. She is deep into her library book of anonymous limericks.

We pick our way through the filmic and literary ruins cavalierly, plucking snippets from here and there, pasting them in, much in the same way as Benjamin saw his work (although we are not aware of Benjamin at the time): a de- and recontextualized collection of quotations.

> The main work consisted in tearing fragments out of their context and arranging them afresh in such a way that they illustrated one another and were able to prove their raison d'être in a free-floating state, as it were. (Arendt 1968)

But no matter how I cast it—consciously in terms of film history, unconsciously in terms more epistemological—Sharon knows we are not working on another *Chariots of Fire* or *Z*. Not even another Marx Brothers film. On the continuum, we are definitely at the low-culture end. Sharon frolics there, recklessly. Distracted, the very real agony and financial disaster of Northwest Arkansas forgotten for the moment, somehow lost in the frenzy of creation, I frolic as well.

Opposition

> The world, he said, was hidden from him by a veil.... The veil was torn, strange to say, in one situation only; and that was at the moment when, as a result of an enema, he passed a motion through his anus. He then felt well again, and for a very short time he saw the world clearly. (Freud 1979, p. 340)

During that summer of writing, first in Little Rock and then on a Florida beach, I feel no stigma, no embarrassment, no queasiness about delving into the baser humors. After all, they are only words, I think then, and if they make people laugh, if they touch a heart string—if they get the picture made—then for me the effort is justified.

For Sharon, it slowly evolves into a different story. Her flirtation with the scatological, her eager embrace of forbidden fruit that she initially finds so seductive, that she plucks with such gusto, loses its allure as it becomes tainted with, among other things, the staleness of familiarity. She wonders if what we are writing is funny, if as an actress she'll be able to say certain words. She argues about adjectives, about nuance and lilt. Her spirit guides appear more often, questioning every scene, reminding her of yoga classes missed, worrying about her "center."

And then her eyes open and she suddenly smells our text for what it is, for what she has helped make it, a judgment that might have been instantaneous to her had she not been a party to its birth.

> Grotesque realism images the human body as multiple, bulging, over- or undersized, protuberant, and incomplete. The openings and orifices of this carnival body are emphasized, not its closure

or finish. It is an image of impure corporeal bulk with its orifices (mouth, flared nostrils, anus) yawning wide and its lower regions (belly, legs, feet, buttocks, and genitals) given priority over its upper regions (head, "spirit," reason). (Stallybrass and White 1986)

In the end, she finds it distasteful. Not, as Noel Coward might say, her cup of tea. Or so I surmise. All Sharon says, on the way to the airport, is, "My head really hurts. Alfred says he doesn't think this kind of thing is good for a gentle soul like me." Alfred is one of her spirit guides, a tiny voice that speaks to her in times of trouble.

> Nymphomaniacal Alice
> Used a dynamite stick for a phallus
> They found her vagina
> In South Carolina
> And her asshole in Buckingham Palace
>
> (Anonymous)

Mattering

With the parallel processes of the expansion of the role of art within consumer culture and the deformation of enclaved art with its separate prestige structure and lifestyle, a blurring of genres and the tendencies toward the deconstruction of hierarchies has occurred. This entails a pluralistic stance toward the variability of taste, a process of cultural de-classification which has undermined the basis of high culture-mass culture distinctions. (Featherstone 1991, p. 25)

President George Bush exhibits a passion for country music. Bill Clinton plays the sax, loves Elvis, and wears baseball caps. Arnold Schwarzenegger and Bruce Willis campaign for Republicans. Jimmy Carter confesses lust. Gore Vidal starts an acting career. Mel Gibson, Richard Gere, and Kenneth Branagh bare their butts in movies—Branagh in a classy production of Shakespeare's *Much Ado About Nothing*.

> A Mob of Metaphors advance,
> Pleas'd with the Madness of the mazy dance:
> How Tragedy and Comedy embrace;
> How Farce and Epic get a jumbled race.
>
> (Pope 1966, p. 65)

> At the market center of the polis we discover a commingling of categories usually kept separate and opposed: centre and periphery, inside and outside, stranger and local, commerce and festivity, high and low.... Only hybrid notions are appropriate to such a hybrid place. (Stallybrass and White 1986, p. 27)

On the maps of what matters, the distinctions between high and low culture are now shrinking hamlets where even Wal-Mart doesn't think it worthwhile to open up shop.[6] A few people, like Sharon, still live in these places. But for most of us, that particular opposition has been mass-media-ized toward a Benjaminian state of ruin. The opposition has been so violated, so ignored, so blurred that it really doesn't matter anymore.

Of course, the resultant vulgarization of the entertainment/ information media and the blurring of other previously sacred boundaries (e.g., between network news and tabloid news) are viewed by some with alarm. But the power rests so firmly elsewhere that, again, those meager voices fall unheard into the void. As a culture, we freely watch with fascination a *Seinfeld* episode on masturbation, all the gross-out episodes of *Beavis and Butt-Head* and *Married with Children*, pictures of mutilated Bosnian children resting easily next to Calvin Klein ads in *Newsweek*, rap artists playing with their crotches, and topless Germans on *Entertainment Tonight*.

To create a paradox, kitsch reigns.

> Kitsch steals motifs and materials at random, regardless of the original ascription of the sources. It takes from classic, modernist, and popular art and mixes all together, becoming in this way the first and foremost recycler. (Olalquiaga 1992)

Kitsch matters and the culture industry knows it. (And so do the political spinmeisters—witness the making, unmaking, and remaking of Bill Clinton.)

Joining

Meagan Morris worries about corporatism and its claim to productivity, security, and efficiency.[7] The idea that government, capital, labor—even ordinary citizens—are all part of a productive entity that is modeled after a corporate team concerns her greatly.

Resistance has no place in this corporate world. Indeed, resistance becomes an archaic concept, a caprice without currency.

A certain clarity comes from looking at the culture industry in corporate terms. It is an industry that people are begging to join, to become part of—this globalized corporate team that entertains, informs, and aestheticizes, making us all into celebrities or, even better, makers of celebrities. The only subversions on the map, the only tactics employed (see de Certeau 1984), are those used to try to get into and remain in the industry, not to resist or subvert it. Such is its hegemonic power and its power of seduction.

The culture industry seduces me, the variety performers, the managers, most of the communications and cultural studies majors in university graduate programs, even for a time the idiosyncratic Sharon. And once we become members of the team, most of our energies are directed toward the benefit of the industry under the fear that we have to produce for the industry to remain a part of it. Most of us cannot resist being seduced by it and once becoming a part of it, apply our cunning toward maintaining our position within it. As an addiction, very little beats it.

Bourdieu calls this expanding group of corporatized dandies "new cultural intermediaries," even "new intellectuals," (Bourdieu 1984, p. 370) defining them as those who

> are engaged in providing symbolic goods and services...the marketing, advertising, public relations, radio and television producers, presenters, magazine journalists, fashion writers, and the helping professions (social workers, marriage counsellors, sex therapists, dieticians, play leaders, etc.). (Featherstone 1991, p. 44)

Add to that actors, movie makers, script writers, variety performers, cabaret artistes.

Stir in aesthetics.

> The increasing sensitivity to aesthetics, style, lifestyle, the stylization of life, and emotional exploration within the new middle class has developed in parallel to a rise in the number of people working as artists and in intermediary art occupations and a more general societal rise in the level of respect that such occupations demand. (Featherstone 1991)

The resulting mix is a powerful brew, a welcoming narcotic that can pass as an opiate for the people.

> Far from "shocking the bourgeoisie" art [becomes] the aesthetic vision of the bourgeoisie. This emphasis [gives] rise to a generation of practitioners, instead of visionaries and innovators. Art [becomes] less elitist and more "professionalized" and "democratic." (Featherstone 1991, p. 46)

> Effectively within the new middle class there may be increasing numbers who accept that the aesthetic life is the ethically good life, that there is no human nature or true self, that we are a collection of quasi-selves, and life is open to be shaped aesthetically. (Featherstone 1991)

The idea that we can be anybody we want to be, that American ideal bludgeoned into our heads since preschool, has suddenly been attacked by a cancer so voracious that it consumes our very beings. And what most of us want to be is on-TV, in-the-movies— a part of the culture industry. Not only celebrities in our own right, but celebrities as our basic right. That we all can't be is the attendant problematic.

We live everywhere already in an "aesthetic" hallucination of reality (Baudrillard 1983b).

Sharon

> Ceaselessly, the devil agitates my ribs
> Surrounding me like an impalpable vapor
> I swallow, and sense him burning in my lungs,

> Filling them with endless, guilty desire.
> ....
> He throws in my eyes, bewildered and deluded,
> Soiled garments, opened wounds,
> And the bloody implements of destruction.

(Baudelaire 1964, p. 145)

The screenplay finished, a wasted Sharon retreats from me and from the project. Months later, she leaves to seek her fortune in New York as a cabaret singer, until now something she has been unable to muster the courage to do. She has some success, performing in clubs like Rainbow and Stars atop Rockefeller Center and being well reviewed in the *New York Times*. She does a tribute to Hillary Clinton at the Waldorf during the Democratic Convention and shines in some of the smaller Washington cabarets. In that rarified, elitist, and shrinking world of the single spotlight, the smoking cigarette, and the half-empty glass of gin, she gains fame for a little while.

Recently, we talk on the phone.

"I am writing a song about fascism," she says from Manhattan. "'The Fascist Rag.' I am very scared, just looking at people on the street. I've seen it all before, in pictures of Berlin in the 1930s. The makeup, the clothes, the blank stares, the sense of ennui."

"Ennui?" I say.

"Ennui," she says.

"I know what you mean," I say, finally.

> Someone condemned, descending without light,
> At the edge of an abyss . . .
> ....
> Where viscous monsters lie waiting
> Their large and phosphorous eyes
> Making the dark night darker still.

(Baudelaire 1964, p. 98)

Anesthesia

As for *East of the 7–11*, it is not well received by agents, producers, actors, or financiers. Everyone hates it, including the variety performers for whom it is written. They don't see themselves that way at all.

The screenplay is never optioned. Another pursuit, another short-lived frolic, another rejection. All quickly filed and forgotten, to linger only in the furthest recesses of memory, as a new adventure takes its place.

> Oh, dear, what can the matter be?
> Oh, dear, what can the matter be?
> Oh, dear, what can the matter be?
> Johnny's so long at the fair.

Notes

1. Modified lyrics by Sharon Douglas.

2. Sung to the Eubie Blake song "I'm Just Wild About Harry." Revised lyrics by Sharon Douglas.

3. Both the Mardi Gras in New Orleans and Carnival in Rio are now heavily regulated and controlled events. With regard to Carnival, as Celeste Olalquiaga (1992) points out in her book *Megalopolis*, authorities built the Sambodromo in 1985 "to control the carnival and its profits" (p. 82). Along with this control comes a certain deflation, a watering-down of carnivalistic essences.

4. The "high" art of European cabaret against the "low" art of exploitation comedy film with its emphasis on the sexual and the scatological. See Stallybrass and White.

5. Susan Buck-Morss (1989) writing about Walter Benjamin's "concepts in their 'extremes' . . . visualized as antithetical polarities that cross each other, revealing a 'dialectical image' at the null point, with its contradictory 'moments' as axial fields" (p. 210).

6. Grossberg in *We Gotta Get Out of This Place* (1992) defines a mattering map as "a socially determined structure of affect which defines the things that do and can matter by those living within the map" (p. 82).

7. In a discussion with students and faculty at the University of Illinois in April 1993, Morris lamented the growth of corporatism, particularly in the United States, and the dedicated, nonadversarial, insistently productive relationship it fosters between employees and the corporation.

Perhaps life appears less agonizing when decentral-ization (and decentering) are no longer understood as chaos or absence—the opposite of presence—but as a marvelous expansion, a multiplicity of independent centers.

—Trinh Minh-ha, *When the Moon Waxes Red*

Home is that place which enables and promotes var-ied and everchanging perspectives, a place where one discovers new ways of seeing reality, frontiers of dif-ference. One confronts and accepts dispersal and frag-mentation as part of the construction of a new world order that reveals more fully where we are, who we can become, an order that does not demand forgetting. "Our struggle is also a struggle of memory against for-getting."

—bell hooks, *Yearning*

4

The Sony's Dying Glow

September on the plains of Illinois. Hot outside, cool inside. Months and miles from the terror of the Ozark epiphany and the failures of Little Rock. The Miss America Pageant is on.

Regis Philbin's words shoot through a forced smile, telling us that sixteen of this year's girls are communication majors, telling Kathie Lee that they're after her job. The audience is poorly miked; the laughter sounds distant and half-hearted.

I balance the bowl on my belly and readjust my pillow.

"Don't you get enough popcorn at the movies?" asks my wife.

I say something about popcorn being therapeutic, about how it is easier to swallow certain absurdities when they are filtered through popcorn, how popcorn makes a movie like *The Player* seem funnier than it really is, that popcorn is the drug of choice for the couch-potato generation.

"Sorry I asked," says my wife.

I say I am sorry I answered.

"Sooner or later you're going to have to get a grip," she says. "You're not the only one, you know."

I am going to ask her what she means by that when Regis announces the semifinalists. He is shorter than all of them, but he has a bounce in his step and the microphone in his hand. The girls are all smiles and nervous giggles. They hug each other.

I say I know I'm not the only one. I say I am sorry.

She smiles at me. She's been smiling at me a lot through the summer. I've been saying I am sorry a lot.

"I like Miss Utah," says my wife. "She's the one who wants to be a tele-evangelist..."

I start thinking about having a meeting, calling up a few people and getting together, just to talk. Some names run through my head. I think about whom I'd invite, and I wonder whether or not they would understand what I am trying to get at. Even if I could get an articulated handle on the idea myself, maybe find words for it in the books that I am now reading for my graduate courses at the university—even then would I be able to get to the heart of this obsession, this thing I am now beginning to characterize as an addiction?

I remember all the people I've met out there, all those like me, who have pursued the same elusive dreams of becoming a part of it all. People who have pursued me, thinking I have a direct pipeline to Hollywood, because I once produced a film with Burt Lancaster and Peter O'Toole. People I let pursue me, because I hope they might have a good script or idea, a galloping horse that I can ride triumphantly back to Hollywood.

It is the most desperate among them who come to mind first.

A vision of Larry floods my brain...

He inches, hat in hand, into the bar of the Capital Hotel in Little Rock. Larry is from Tulsa, a short, fat man, maybe twenty-five, in a K-Mart suit, polyester tie, and plastic shoes. Larry and a group of his friends spent all their money, seventy-five thousand dollars, making *Mutilations*, a feature-length horror film written and directed by Larry, with special effects by somebody who once knew Ray Harryhausen. A moment from the film comes to mind: A dirty tea kettle, flung by someone just off camera, tumbles through the air and lands on the ground. It's supposed to be a spaceship. From the spout, a badly animated toy store monster covered in Vaseline walks out, roars, and spits sparks. Off camera, people scream. A month before, Larry asks me to sell the film, and I agree, thinking the movie might have some video value, good for a few campy yuks, so bad that it's good. I find out I am wrong. Nobody I know in LA or New York or London wants the film, and I tell Larry straight out, that evening in the Capital Hotel Bar. Larry doesn't say anything for a while, doesn't touch his Diet

7Up. His face turns quietly red under his greased-down blond hair. Finally he says, "I'll sell mail order if I have to, out of my garage if I have to, and then I'll make another one and sell it the same way, until they take notice of me. Modesty forbids me to say it, Mr. Kohn, but I will anyway: Hollywood hasn't seen the last of me." He fidgets, bites his lower lip. Then his eyes light up. "Hey," he says, suddenly eager again. "Do you think maybe you could get Roger Ebert to look at it?"

And I remember Joe, on the phone from LA, somebody else's phone, somebody else's dime. I take the call in the bathtub. It is 8:30 a.m. in Little Rock, 6:30 a.m. in LA, as I listened to his Texas twang, talking fast. "The kids are having a rough time making friends—their clothes are all wrong. Sylvia's got a job substitute teaching a couple days a month, and I'm working nights at a Dairy Queen. Reason for the call, though, is I've got a new treatment, called *Highway 41 South*, a perfect vehicle for James Woods. Didn't you say you knew how to get to him? Can you? I can drop it off anywhere in LA anytime before Friday. On Friday the guy comes to pick up the car. I had to sell it to pay the rent. Make a few calls, will you, and get back to me. Time's kinda running out . . . "

And of course David, from the car phone, this time on his way to some party on the Vineyard, always trying to buy his way into every deal. New York suburbs, rich (but not rich enough) daddy, balding, nasal, pushy, sex-starved David. David, chattering fast, trying to sound like he knows what he's talking about: "Hey, Sumner Redstone's—owns Viacom and Showtime, you know— Sumner's a friend of mine. He'll write a check, finance the whole film, P and A and all. I mean, I can get the package to him at the right level. You know the Bronfman family? I get to Sumner through them. My deal is 8 percent finder's fee, executive producer credit, most-favored-nation salary, and points clauses. And I get to be on the set and Rutger has to know who I am and what I did. Deal? Just put it all in a letter and fax it to me and we're in business."

And financier Diane Valentine of the syrupy voice and the hair-in-her-eyes coyness. "Let me have your FedEx number and I'll send the script to Jean-Jacques at Crédit Lyonnais. He's close, real close, he'll do it for me. Lord knows, I've done enough for that bastard. And then you can come to New York and buy me lunch at Felidia's and we'll celebrate . . . "

And Harry the writer, still writing, still phoning, still hoping, still eating. He always has food in his mouth when he talks. "The fuckers at William Morris are beating my door down. Holbrook got 'em to read some of my stuff. They're flying me out, right after the strike's over."

And Tod, the man who came up with the idea for Sam's Wholesale Club for Wal-Mart. Tod, now a quarter of a million poorer thanks to me and the fiasco in Northwest Arkansas, now smitten with the business despite his heavy financial loss. He's heard from some guys in Nashville. "Their idea sounds good, a singing cowboy film, you know, like Gene Autry. Paul Williams is going to write the music and Rex Allen Jr.'s involved. They need fifty thousand dollars development money. I'm gonna give it to 'em, but this time I wanna be protected. Do you have a good contract my lawyer could, you know, copy some clauses from?"

And Furnivall, the retired British secret service agent, who has access to money in Hong Kong and Zimbabwe; Meredith, the New Orleans set decorator with a closetful of scripts about lost loves; Mitch, a National Guard major, whose one script, a Vietnam story called *I Kill For Peace*, was optioned twice in twelve years but never made; Rita, six years of New York actor's workshops, four of therapy, and three local commercials to show for it; Claire, the dancer, who traveled to LA eight times in five years only to find that her high school sweetheart, now an LA record company president, wouldn't take her calls, not once; and me, two decades older, a hundred thousand dollars poorer, two movies made, three scripts sold, at least fifty deals almost done, now wondering what it all means—wondering what I've done with my life, what I'll do with the rest of it.

There are twenty years filled with people. And there are thousands more out there as well, all incapable of giving up, most living lives that are "only temporary," making do however they can in case they are summoned—sell the script, get the part, be selected as a game show contestant. Could any of those people be feeling the same things that I am? Is it at all possible that others might be questioning the lure of the culture industry and how it affects their lives?

I stick a handful of popcorn in my mouth.

"Did you see this?" asks my wife. She is reading *Entertainment Weekly*.

On the screen, the field of Miss America contenders narrows to five, three of them communications majors.

"See what?" I say, looking over her shoulder and following her finger to a point on the magazine page.

She reads out loud. "Jim Mullen's Hot Sheet. Number 13. 'Nobel Prize. It's nice, but it's not like getting your star on Hollywood's Walk of Fame.' "

This time she doesn't have to smile. I swear she can read my mind. She always knows. Sometimes, she knows before I know.

Commercials come and go and, finally, a future TV personality with a bachelor's degree in communications is crowned the winner.

"Miss Utah should have left out the evangelist part," says my wife. "She scared the judges with that. She should have said she wanted to be just like Julie Moran or Mary Hart. That would have been better."

Regis and Kathie Lee start singing, "There she is, Miss America . . . There she is, my ideal . . . "

"So?" my wife says.

"I-Wanna-Be-In-Pictures Anonymous," I say. "IWBPA. I'm going to get a core group together. We're going to have meetings and admit our addiction, confront our obsession, and together we're going to beat it, one day at a time. There will be regular meetings in movie theater basements and video stores all across the country. We'll make PSA announcements. PhD dissertations will be written. Celebrities will start to come as well and discover that they, too, are victims of this addiction, that you don't have to be a failure to be hooked. People will look inward and start to lead productive lives again. And I'll be remembered as a kind of prophet, as the one who started it all."

My wife looks me. The expression on her face tells me nothing.

"What?" I say.

Miss America is crying, her face streaked with that unique mixture of tears and mascara. This is her moment, her rite of passage, when she becomes a part of it all.

"You'll be famous," my wife says. "They'll make a movie of your life."

"I'm serious," I say.

"So am I," she says. "I'll play me and Daniel Day-Lewis will play you."

"I'm onto something here," I say. "I'm discovering something worthwhile here . . . "

"Sure you are," she says.

"Don't you remember all those people in Arkansas?" I say. "The looks on their faces when the production collapsed, like I'd personally sentenced them to death or something, derailed their personal train to Hollywood. I mean, my God, isn't there something else—anything else—in their lives?"

"Is there anything else in yours?" she says.

"That's my point," I say. "That's what I'm talking about. There must be, but I can't see it, hard as I try. Elusive little devil, that 'anything else' . . . "

"Well," she says. "Well and golly gee."

"Help me, here," I say. "Please."

She commandeers the remote control and clicks off the TV. The room goes black. The bowl somehow falls off my stomach when she rolls over to me. Popcorn spills everywhere. We cavort for a while among the kernels, in the Sony's dying glow.

Where does the tragedy first of all take place? In the body, in the stomach, in the legs, as we know since the Greek tragedies. Aeschylus' characters tell, first and foremost, a body state. Myself—I realized this afterwards—I began by carrying out a rehabilitation of these body states since they are so eloquent, since they concretely speak of the troubles of our souls. In this area I work under the microscope, as a spiritual anatomist.

—Helene Cixous, *Helene Cixous Reader*

The locus of addictiveness cannot be the substance itself and it can scarcely even be the body itself, but must
be some over-arching abstraction that governs the narrative relations between them.

—Eve Kosofsky Sedgwick, "Epidemics of the Will"

Clear expression, often equated with correct expression, has long been the criterion set forth in treatises
on rhetoric, whose aim was to order discourse so as to
persuade. The language of Taoism and Zen, for example, which is perfectly accessible but rife with paradox
does not qualify as "clear" (paradox is "illogical" and
"nonsensical" to many Westerners), for its intent lies
outside the realm of persuasion.

—Trinh Minh-ha, *Woman, Native, Other*

5

My Elusive Dreams

Around midnight. Class tomorrow. A country station on the radio, a fifth-generation Xerox of C. Wright Mills in my hand, the TV turned down low, a bottle of ginger ale on the nightstand, my wife asleep beside me.

> The media have not only filtered our experience of external realities, they have also entered into our very experience of ourselves. They have provided us with new identities and aspirations of what we should like to be... C. Wright (Mills 1956, p. 67)

Travis Tritt on the radio now. The song is "Lord Have Mercy on the Working Man."

> More than that: (1) the media tell the man in the mass who he is—they give him identity; (2) they tell him what he wants to be—they give him aspirations; (3) they tell him how to get that way—they give him technique; (4) they tell him how to feel that he is that way even when he is not—they give him escape. C. Wright On (Mills 1956, p. 68)

Then I think: Did he sing, "They're building me for killing me?"

Then the phone rings.

"Wellllll..." Harry's raspy voice. "Long time, hey..."

"Harry."

"Country on the radio? You?" His laugh turns into a cough. Harry was born with a heart problem. He almost died when he was eighteen. Surgeons in Houston operated and saved his life. Only problem was that they sliced a nerve to his vocal chords in the process. He's talked with a rasp ever since. And the cigarettes don't help.

"It's real late here, Harry. Where are you?"

"I'm back on Long Island, out in East Hampton, staying at Jinx Falkenberg's old place. Woody Harrelson just bought it. He's letting me break it in for him. Soooo . . . "

I reach for the remote control and ease up the volume. Bob Berkowitz is interviewing three people on CNBC. Two fat women with blunt hair occupy the ends of a sofa. Sandwiched between them is a skinny guy with a complexion problem. The words across the bottom of the screen read "People Who Enjoy Ménage à Trois."

" . . . I was just thinking," says Harry, "this thing's come up, a guy in New York who's a friend of a guy I met out here at the beach, he just read *Arkansas Spring* and he's interested. Thinks I'm a fucking great writer. Then I thought, maybe, well, maybe enough time's passed since Arkansas, maybe I could bring you back into this thing. The guy's worth about a hundred fifty million and he's got a production company. His partner in LA has been steering him up to now, a real asshole. Burke, that's my friend out here, says there's a good chance we can short-circuit him, get right in there with *Arkansas Spring* as the first project, go on from there—"

On the TV, Bob Berkowitz wants to know what's so exciting about ménage à trois. He asks the question on the TV.

"Well, ummmm," says the girl on the right.

"It's just kinda . . . you know . . . " says the girl on the left.

"Hey, man, jeez, like, ain't it, like, plain as the nose on your face?" The boy in the middle chortles as he talks.

"What you drinking, Harry?"

"Nothing much, a glass of wine."

"Harry—"

"This guy's pure Park Avenue. We need you to go in and talk to him with us. Sell the thing. You know how to answer the hard questions. In there without you, I'll drop ash on my tie and piss in my pants. Speaking metaphorically, of course."

I hear the click of a cigarette lighter.

"Burke'll send you a ticket, we already talked about it. There's a fee in it for you, five hundred or so, and maybe something on the picture, coproducer credit, a couple of points, maybe the LA asshole's job if he likes you."

"Damn it, Harry—"

"What you doing out there, anyhow? I lived in Iowa once. Taught at the Writer's Workshop. Iowa anywhere near Illinois?"

"I'm trying to give it up, Harry."

CNBC goes to commercial and I flip over to HBO. Kevin Costner is standing in a corn field.

"I did that a couple of times. Went into advertising once. Edited a literary magazine at Memphis State. Wrote an article once called 'Academia Sucks.' "

A baseball player evaporates into thin air.

"Have you seen *Field of Dreams*?"

"'Build it and they will come?' Didn't it win an award? Biggest Piece of Horseshit of 1989? I mean, Jesus Christ Almighty what a piece of horseshit."

"Yeah, I know." I flip on.

"Did you see *Glengarry Glen Ross*?" says Harry. "Now that's a fucking masterpiece. Talk about depressing. I mean, Mamet, Christ, the words. He really got inside those suckers. And Jack Lemmon, fucking hell! Did you see it?"

"Kind of reminded me of the movie business."

"Everything's the movie business. That's what you don't understand. We can't escape it; we were born into it, our generation, it's us, for better or for worse. Take Binky, you remember Binky, my son the waiter?"

"Uh huh."

"He got fired from his production job at MGM and is back at the Palm. He says it's not like it used to be, when they were dealing coke out of the bar and half the agents in LA hung out there, but he's making contacts, the only reason he took the job, making contacts. Binky's started writing scripts now, like his old man. Pretty good, too."

"What are you eating, Harry?"

"You fucker," he says. "I can't get away with anything with you, can I?" A laugh, a choking sound, a cough.

"You're always eating, Harry. Your moustache is always full of food. I can hear it dripping on the telephone."

"Sauerbraten. Marinated it myself. Left over from yesterday lunch, warmed in the microwave. Bet you wish you were here."

On CNN they are running the tape of Bill Clinton playing the saxophone on the *Arsenio Hall Show*. Bill thrusts his pelvis forward, leans back and blows, sunglasses shading his eyes. The place is swinging. Arsenio's teeth are blinding. The voice-over says something about today being National Saxophone Day.

A voice on the radio sings about love, mushrooms, and dung. Lyrics again. The country station. Some singer with a name that sounds like Chevis Tritt.

"You ever hear of Chevis Tritt?"

"Travis," says Harry, "Travis Tritt. Country singer. Chevis is a scotch whiskey. Tritt's strictly moonshine. Sorta the new David Allen Coe. Met him once in Nashville. Coe, that is. A jug of sour mash in one hand and a buxom cutie in the other. Come on, man, what do you say?"

"I don't know, Harry. I'm really trying here."

"What in God's name are you doing that's so goddam important? Going to school? Man, I've been there. It's not where it's happening. It's wank time, man."

"There are some aspects—"

"You're the Ayatollah, for Christ's sake. Sitting in exile in Illinois, reading the classics—you know, *Casablanca*, *Grand Illusion*, *Breathless*, *Vertigo*, *White Heat*—waiting for the revolution, waiting to be summoned from your temporary think tank, your impermanent ivory tower, your bogus bolt hole, to take your rightful place—"

"Stop it, Harry."

"I know. Don't get carried away. But, metaphor becomes me. You should have been here. I almost stood up, it sounded so good. I almost thought about writing it down."

"I don't know, Harry...I mean, I'm just starting to get used to this school thing, on doing some serious work, for a change. I'm actually thinking about stuff other than box office grosses. Me...It's pretty scary sometimes..."

"*It's a Wonderful Life*," says Harry. "Jimmy Stewart, remember that? You're turning into a Jewish Jimmy Stewart."

"Soppy, manipulative drivel, Harry," I hear myself saying too quickly. "*Rear Window* was a lot better. And remember him in *Two Rode Together* with Richard Widmark? John Ford without John Wayne. I just saw it for about the thirtieth time. Now that's a Jimmy Stewart I wouldn't mind becoming."

"Wouldn't mind becoming?" says Harry. "Jesus H. Christ. Come on, man, shake off the fucking academic cobwebs. Do this little thing for me. Get them pistons pumping again. You don't have anything to lose and you got everything to gain. It's in your blood; it's in everybody's blood. How's that for good writing? Fucking cliché city, for God's sake."

"How's the wine holding out, Harry?"

"Fine. A Vallejo 1991. Vintage stuff."

"I don't know if I could, Harry, seriously, practically."

"It hasn't changed at all. Everybody's still an asshole. The same bullshit still applies. You look so fucking honest. That's why everybody believes you. Give the money to the quiet guy. The important things don't change."

"Everything changes, Harry. The first rule of postmodern life. But, that's not what I mean. It's this PhD thing, the classes, the readings. They've stolen my words. They take words and redefine them. Not satisfied with that, they make up completely new meanings for them, all in the name of epistemology and shifting paradigms. I can't say anything anymore like I believe it, because I don't. They're taking conviction away from me. I mean, everything's relative, contextual, interactional, deferred—"

I take a sip of ginger ale, now eager to talk.

"I can hear that ol' cocoon starting to crack," says Harry.

In a rush, me, continuing: "It began last year with Jim Carey, the communications dean. He lectured on ideology. After he was done, I had no idea what it meant anymore, and I haven't been able to use it since. The word *ideology*, that is. He did it to *culture*, too. And *communication*. This year, Denzin, he's a sociologist, has robbed me of *data* and *why* and *subject* and *object* and he's working on *voyeur*. Only he talks mostly about *voyeurism*. The 'ism' makes it an ideology, I guess, and that's double trouble. Then there's Baudrillard, Mr. Postmodern. He's stolen *seduction* and *simulation* and *simulacrum* which, admittedly, I didn't really use a whole hell of a lot. But, along with *simulation* went *stimulation*, for reasons I can't fully understand. So, you see, without the words, where am I? Who am I going to convince of anything?"

"'The simulacrum is never that which conceals the truth—it is the truth which conceals that there is none. The simulacrum is true.' That simulacrum?" says Harry.

"You asshole," I say, and flip off the TV.

"Who says a writer can't read."

"How long will it take?"

"One or two meetings. Three days at the most. You can stay with Constance. She still has the apartment off Canal Street. Hell, Pam'll love a couple of days in New York."

I look over to her. She's stirs, rolls over, curls up. She is smiling in her sleep.

"How is she? How's the kid? What is she now, three? What's her name, again?"

"Harry—"

"Yeah?"

"Fax me a letter outlining the deal. Maybe your friend Burke could get a lawyer to draw it up. The words to keep in mind are 'generous but fair.'"

"You won't regret it," says Harry.

"It's only a couple of days, Harry. Try to schedule it over a weekend so I don't miss class."

"Hey, kid. It'll be great. The fax'll go out tomorrow."

"'Bye, Harry."

The cradle reaches up and grabs the phone from my hand. My palm is clammy. The only sounds in the room are the ticking of a clock, the breathing of my wife, and Charlie Rich on the radio, his voice filled with silver, singing "My Elusive Dreams."

I let C. Wright Mills slip to the floor. I wait for sleep to come. The fax never arrives.

Perhaps the term "neuroasthenia" applies here, since the *flaneur* does not seem to touch reality with direct confidence but with "fingertips that are immediately withdrawn."

—Weinstein and Weinstein, "Georg Simmel: Sociological Flaneur Bricoleur"

Often I felt as though I was in a trance at my typewriter, that the shape of a particular memory was decided not by my conscious mind but by all that is dark and deep within me, unconscious but present. It was the act of making it present, bringing it into the open, so to speak, that was liberating.

—bell hooks, *Talking Back, Thinking Feminist, Thinking Black*

6

So to Speak

On the phone, staring at the computer screen, then at a yellowing book of poetry in my hand. Purple crayon scribbles decorate the pages of the dog-eared garage sale acquisition. Into the mouth piece, brushing it lightly with my lips as I speak, I say, "Hey, listen to this . . . "

And I quote, in a monotone, as is my manner:

> "I think, no matter where you stray,
> That I shall go with you a way.
> Though you may wander sweeter lands,
> You will not soon forget my hands,
> Nor yet the way I held my head,
> Nor all the tremulous things I said.
> You still will see me, small and white
> And smiling, in the secret night,
> And feel my arms about you when
> The day comes fluttering back again.
> I think, no matter where you be,
> You'll hold me in your memory
> And keep my image, there without me,
> By telling later loves about me."
>
> (Parker 1994, p. 156)

"That's funny." It is Trix on the other end of the phone, Trix in New York, Trix of the burgundy hair and green eyes and long legs and nervous laugh, Trix of the trade. As I like to say.

"Dorothy Parker."

"She's funny. Is she dead?"

I hear the cats at the other end of the long-distance line and picture them as I last saw them: one black, one blood orange, both perched on a too-often-painted window ledge below a pane laced with limp rain, their yellow cat eyes languidly watching a naked man do a ragged barre in the window across Eldridge Street. The Lower East Side. The East Village.

"You still love New York?" I say.

"Aach, well, you know, it's not Cape Town," she says.

"No place is," I say. "Not even Cape Town."

"I know," she says. "Sad, don't you think?"

"I imagine it's not as bad as they say. Nothing is ever as bad, or as simple, as they say, or so they say."

I hear a tiny plop of water over the phone, like the sound of a single drop of rain landing unexpectedly on my cheek just before a torrential downpour.

"And you," says Trix, "what are you doing when you're not reading women poetry over the phone?"

"Not much. Languishing might be a good word. Waiting for the cells to regenerate after the lobotomy."

On the computer screen I type my login and password and enter the world of electronic mail. On the screen come those four words that I now cherish: "You have new mail."

"You miss it, huh," says Trix. "The thrill of it. I can tell . . ."

I hear her light a cigar, a little one, short and stubby like a cigarette, but dark brown and sweet, made in Germany; the brand name is Al Capone Pockets, and they come in a cheap black paper packet. I know. A friend of mine sends them to her from Munich. People send Trix things.

"You have to remember something to miss it," I say.

"You remember the film business. You remember every fucking thing," she says. "I hate it, too."

"Memory?" I say.

"The film business," she say. "Memory, too."

The sound of a deep draw and a slow exhalation and a sigh.

"David Heller," she says, "called the other day and wanted me to go to a meeting at William Morris with him. I couldn't believe it. There's some fucker he wants to impress, some agent for god's sake, and he thinks it makes him seem more important, more significant, if I'm dangling from his arm. He told me to wear something black and slinky and not to forget the boots. I told him to go fuck himself."

"Short, bald, Jewish men are a dime a dozen," I say. "Tall, exotic, cigar-smoking South African models who know how to say fuck are not."

"Fuck off," she says.

My e-mail is something from Sandra, from Texas.

Trix says, "You know I mean that in a nice way."

"I know," I say.

"I mean," she says, "the smarmy little bastard. Jake also used to take me along to meetings. I absolutely hated it. He'd beam and call me 'Babe' and say I inspired him when he wrote whatever piece of shit he was peddling and the rich bastards would gawk and drool, like I was supper or something."

"Jake," I said.

"My dearly beloved soon-to-be-ex-husband."

"Have you heard from him?" I ask.

"He had dinner with Tim Leary again last night. At his house in the Hollywood Hills. Imagine a movie about Timothy Leary's life. Jake's supposed to write it for Disney or somebody now. They want to make it before Leary dies and his brain is shot into orbit. They've given Jake his first check already."

"Jesus Christ," I say. "Imagine a movie about The Doors. Or Jack Ruby. Or Jimmy Hoffa, for God's sake. Jack Nicholson as Hoffa, directed by Danny DeVito. A Beverly Hills squirrel builds another icon. Look at what *JFK* did to history. Look at what these movies are doing to me. Look at me. Look. Just look, period. Preferably from afar."

"Calm down," says Trix. "It'll be all right."

"Pardon me," I say, "for being reductionist."

"Pardon me for living," says Trix. "Fucking assholes, every last one of them."

"I know," I say.

"Assholes," she says.

"Except me," I say, "when I was trying to be one of them. Except me."

"You can sound like an asshole," she says. "When you want to."

I look at Sandra's message, white letters on a black screen.

"You hide in language. Not when one encounters you in person. Or at least not when I encounter you in person. Strip it down. Art sucks when it is enigmatic. Say what you think without decoration. Then, when it occurs, the decoration will be a surprise, a delight, a gem. But I guess you must encounter the world on your own terms. I wouldn't like it if you tried to tell me what to do. Adieu. S."

"I'm seeing the frogman again," says Trix.

"The frogman?" I say.

"You know," she says, "the one who had the performance anxiety problem, the one who took the AIDS test with me, the one after the male model from Milan and before the photographer with the PhD in philosophy, the one who tried too hard or should I say tried too soft. You know, the one who couldn't get it up on Labor Day."

"The entertainment lawyer," I say. "He's not from France, he just looks like a frog. But a handsome frog."

"That's the one," she says. "See, you do have a memory, for the important things."

"Your prince."

"My prince the frogman. He's better now. We're finally sort of intimate but, you know, we don't actually do it. We do it but don't do it. It's easier for him. Satisfaction is achieved."

"I'm confused," I say. "What is it that you actually do, then? What does 'sort of intimate' mean? I mean, I know it must be difficult, having a sex life in New York these days. But, how are you intimate? How do you not do it? I'm confused."

Trix laughs. There is a dull pop and the gurgle of liquid being poured coming over the phone line.

"You want me to tell you," she says, "don't you? You want details. You're so fucking curious."

"I am," I say. "I can't help it."

"A fucking voyeur."

"A theoretical voyeur," I say. "There's a distinction."

"Uh-huh."

"I mean," I say, "how can you do something by not doing it? How can you be a part of something like the sex act, you know, without—"

"Aach, man," she says. "We just sort of lie there, close, but not really touching, and I do my thing and he does his thing and we watch each other and we talk to each other, you know, softly and intimately, and it's nice and then sometimes we come and sometimes we even come together. Afterwards, maybe we hug and go to sleep. Fluids never mix."

"I did that in high school," I say. "I think. With the guys in the car, probably. We would have skipped the hugging and sleeping parts."

"It's New York in the 1990s," she says. "What can I say? I'm not going to let the fucker fuck me now, even if he could manage it. It just isn't worth it."

"The show," I say, "isn't worth the price of admission. Ends don't justify means. Ends don't justify ends. No matter what you do, you run the risk of getting burned or getting killed. Nothing is worth it, anymore."

"You're always so dramatic," she says. "So upbeat. It's part of your charm."

"On the other hand," I say, "you could also be doing it right now, while you're talking to me."

"I could," says Trix. "But I don't think I am."

I hear another water sound, a splash this time, a more confident whoosh followed by a short gurgle, like the signature sound of a perfect dive.

"I mean," I say, "if you can figure out a way of doing it, of engaging the world without actually leaving the house, of achieving recognition and satisfaction without having to suffer human-to-human interaction . . . "

"Believe me," says Trix, "simultaneous masturbation is a pretty sucky substitute."

I hear her draw deeply on her cigar.

"Masturbation," she says. "But you probably know as much as I do about that."

"Probably," I say.

"It really does suck," she says. "But what's a girl to do?"

I am still staring at the computer screen.

"Do you," I say, "think I hide in language?"

"You're hiding in Illinois," says Trix.

"I guess," I say. "But I have relapses. I have visions—sort of like hot flashes—of what it used to be like, of lounging around the pool at the Beverly Hills Hotel or having a drink on top of the Bel Age or, say, ordering cold pheasant at the Groucho Club in London with Julie Christie. I also talk to you. And I talk to Jake."

"Just my luck," says Trix. "The little fellow finds success two months after I leave him."

"I know ..." I say. "The gloat in his voice. 'I'm lunching with Arthur Penn ...' That kind of irritating shit."

"It's fate," she says. "It wasn't mean to be. I believe that. But it's okay. I'm lying here in my bath with my glass of champagne and my cigars and my cats and it's okay. I'm better off without the fucker. Wouldn't you say?"

I start typing a reply to Sandra.

"what'd i say to piss you off? ... dancing with words doesn't mean i'm hiding in them ... i love words ... words are all i have ... all any of us ever have ..."

"Are your breasts," I say, "floating?"

"My breasts are too small to float," she says. "Either that, or they're always floating. Why?"

"I was just curious," I say. "Well, not really curious. I just thought it'd be fun to ask."

"Asshole," says Trix. "So, should I take acting lessons after my aerobics class on Thursdays? I can act better than, oh, say, Greta Garbo."

I look at the clock in the corner of my computer screen. It says 2:27 a.m. It's an hour later in New York.

"It's a shitty business," I say. "It about killed me. Figuratively and literally. Once this guy in Arkansas said he was going home to get his gun. He said it when I took his job away from him. I wrecked his dream, he said. And he went home to get his gun. I was scared shitless."

"But you still love it," says Trix. "In spite of all that. You can't help it. Nobody can help it. I mean, what else is there, when you get right down to it? Going to medical school? Working as a fucking cab driver?"

"You can't love something you don't understand," I say. "All you can do is try to figure it out, knowing you never will, but also knowing you can never stop."

"What kind of bullshit's that?" she says.

"Philosophical bullshit," I say.

And then I start typing the words as a speak them to Trix.

"You're no longer in charge of your own dreams . . . "

A smile flits briefly across my face. I type a little faster as I say, "You become, among other things, an ambivalence chaser."

And then my smile fades, as if it had never been there at all.

"You do," says Trix, "hide in language. As well as in Illinois."

"You remember the Peggy Lee song," I say, "'Is That All There Is, Is That All There Is to Love . . . ' Something like that. I can't sing it. I can't sing. You remember it?"

"No," says Trix.

"Well," I say, "it doesn't matter; it doesn't really apply, anyway."

"So when are you coming to New York?" she says. "David Heller'd love to see you, take you to lunch at the Gotham Bar and Grill and pretend he left his wallet at home, maybe introduce you to his friend at William Morris as somebody famous from a faraway place."

I can hear her smiling on the other end of the phone. I can hear the cats smiling, too.

"Okay," I say, "I'll lighten up. I'll get a grip."

"Not on me you won't," she says.

"Well, then," I say, "I'll get a grip on me then, maybe. Following your lead."

"You fucker," she says.

"I'm learning from you," I say. "You're teaching me."

The sound of multiple sirens suddenly pierces the New York night, so loud that we stop talking until the cacophony subsides.

"I was thinking," she says, "that you could send me some dirt."

"Dirt?" I say.

"You know, dirt," she says, "earth, from the ground, what flowers grow in. Dirt."

"What," I say, "do you want with dirt?"

"I eat it," she says. "The blacker the better. I always used to eat dirt in South Africa, but I'm afraid to eat New York dirt. It's too, you know, polluted—"

"Too dirty."

"That, too," she says. "But, can you, seriously? I'd love some. I hear you have really good dirt in Illinois."

"Sure," I say, "I can. But why? I mean, why do you eat dirt?"

"I love the taste of it," she says. "The texture of it. I like the feel of it in my mouth. The way it settles in my stomach. I just love it. I always have. I miss it."

"Okay," I say. "I will."

"Thanks," she says.

I hear her yawn and imagine her settling deeper into the tub.

"Be reckless," I say. "Take the acting class. Have Jake introduce you to some agents and directors in LA. Go for it. What the hell, why not. Just don't get any more addicted than you are already. Don't take it seriously. Try to be a part of it all without being a part of it all. You know, like making love to the frogman."

"Yeah," she says, "well, shit."

"I know," I say. "Easier said than done . . ."

I hear her rummaging, undoubtedly for another cigar, her purse above her head, the phone crooked between her ear and her shoulder, things probably falling in the bath water.

I type some more to Sandra.

". . . but you're right . . . surprises are good . . . enigmas are bad . . . unfortunately, enigmas are all we have and, since we've seen it all, surprises are few and far between . . . how's that for closure? . . . or is it foreclosure? . . . as baudrillard once said, 'we live everywhere already in an aesthetic hallucination of reality.' . . . ciao, n."

"And you," says Trix, "what about you?"

"I'm okay," I say, "I'm getting there. Maybe listening to you thickly describe the sordid details of your life is thrill enough, for me, for now."

"Shut up," says Trix. "And stop making fun of me. I'm not a bad girl, you know."

"You're as good as they come," I say. "When they come. If they come together."

"Jesus," says Trix. "You never stop."

"I know," I say. "But I do try, from time to time, from place to place. Maybe that's why I'm in Illinois. Want to hear another poem?"

"Do I have a choice?"

"Dorothy Parker again," I say, "A former writing partner of mine introduced me to her in Little Rock a long time ago."

And I read to Trix from the yellowing page:

> "My heart went fluttering with fear
> Lest you should go, and leave me here
> To beat my breast and rock my head
> And stretch me sleepless on my bed.
> Ah, clear they see and true they say
> That one shall weep, and one shall stray
> For such is Love's unvarying law . . .
> I never thought, I never saw
> That I should be the first to go;
> How pleasant that it happened so!"
>
> (Parker 1994, p. 135)

"That's it?" says Trix. "Is that all there is?"

"That's it," I say. "For now, so to speak."

In the discos, which reproduce very closely the old movie palace effects, dancers like to be alone on the floor . . . alone in the middle of the crowd, protected by the amplifying action of 7,000 watts and by laser rays.

—Paul Virilio, *The Aesthetics of Disappearance*

As the philosopher Gilles Deleuze remarks, our civilization is not one of image, but rather, a civilization of the cliché. We often read images on the level of metaphors and perceive meaning as something there, already existing. What seems more difficult is to see an image as image, without metaphors, with its excess, its radical or unjustifiable character. To find again, to restore all that one does not see in the image is not simply to parody the cliché or to correct it. Rather it implies disturbing the comfort and security of stable meaning that leads to a different conception of montage, of framing and reframing in which the notions of time and of movement are redefined, while no single reading can exhaust the dimensions of the image.

—Trinh Minh-ha, *The Moon Waxes Red*

7

Among Other Things

Johnny Depp on addiction: "If I could have another mouth grafted onto my face to smoke more, I would do it."

I'm in a waiting room. Exotic fish in a tank, herbal remedies in a locked glass case, an old man in a chair across from me. I glance up from the *US Magazine* in my lap. The man looks like Wilfred Brimley in the Quaker Oats commercials. He is staring at me.

I say, "I met Wilfred Brimley once."

"That a fact," says the man. "Some folks tell me there's a resemblance."

"Some folks," I say, "are right."

"I been takin' steel guitar lessons," he says. "I can do a pretty good rendition of 'Your Cheatin' Heart.'"

The clock on the wall clicks over to 10:05. Jane's five minutes late.

Tommy Lee Jones on fame. He seems to think it is twisted, alienating, without grace.

"You," the old man says to me, "in show biz? Hear tell there's a young fella comes in here's in show biz. Any chance you'd be that fella?"

"No," I say, "I don't think so. I don't think I am."

"You wouldn't be here incognito, would you?" he says. "Folks look like you ain't got no need comin' here, less'n you like pamperin'. Ain't no doc sent you here. That's what let me to suspectin'."

Tori Spelling on why she can't go to Disneyland anymore. Too many fans bother her too much.

"Just because I said I met Wilfred Brimley once," I say, "doesn't necessarily make me a William Morris agent; it doesn't make me that fella who comes in here. If indeed there is such a fella. If indeed I really did meet Wilfred Brimley once. If indeed, indeed."

"I was just," he says, "askin'."

"There are relations in this world," I say, "but there are no necessary relations."

"You ain't," the old man says, "met my cousin Elwood."

I lie naked on the table, my groin is covered by a small towel, my head rests on a cervical pillow, my eyes stare at glitter glued to the ceiling, Patsy Cline sings, Jane's thumb works the side of my big toe.

Patsy dances in my brain, falling to pieces at the sight of me.

I say, "And then what happened?"

Jane says, "Then the girl says, 'Here, you won't be needing this!' and reaches right into Bart's chest and pulls his heart out. It's still pumping blood. She throws it onto the floor of the tree house. It continues to pump, bouncing around like a blind red frog. Then she leaves on a motorcycle with the other guy. Poor Bart. It was really very funny."

"Sorry I missed it," I say. "*The Simpsons* strikes a chord with me. I wish to God they didn't. I mean, there are certain things you shouldn't laugh at, no matter how funny there are."

I close my eyes to see Patsy watching me walk by, a new girl on my arm, as I fail to notice her, still falling to pieces.

"I was rolling," she says, "on the floor. Mike had to pick me up and put me back in the chair."

"He did that for you?"

"He did," she says. "He's so much stronger since he started law school."

"Law school?" I say.

"He doesn't want to be a writer anymore," she says. "He wants to be a lawyer. Like his brother. He wants to be a lawyer so he can help people who can't afford lawyers. He's entering a different time warp now. He likes it better than the old one. I mean, he can't write for shit. Remember his novel, wimpy self-indulgent drivel."

"As I recall," I say, "spelling wasn't his strong suit."

"Helping old ladies and kids," she says, "that's what he does best."

"And dogs."

"And dogs."

The swell of Patsy's voice, the soaring ache, as I imagine her dreaming of my sweet touch.

"All the graduates of Harvard Law School want to be comedy writers now," I say. "It says so in this week's *Newsweek*. Hundred-thousand-dollar educations and they want to write for *Beavis and Butt-Head*."

"Give me," says Jane, "strength."

"You have it," I say. "You're the strongest person I know. You're like the strong man in the circus. You can bend steel with your bare hands. You bend me with your bare hands all the time."

"Careful," she says, "or I'll bend things not intended to be bent."

What is it about Patsy Cline, telling me to hurt her now, to get it over, her raw cry now hurting me?

"Speaking of strength," I say, "Trix called from New York the other day."

"Trix," says Jane.

"Trix of the trade," I say. "The South African model who lives in the East Village. She got in a fight yesterday. Seems she was walking down the steps into the subway, on her way up-town for a shoot or something, and this guy in a suit and tie passed her. He glanced over at her, looked at her with absolute hatred, said something like, "You fucking bitch," and then he spit on her. No reason. She didn't know him. He just spit in her face."

"New York," says Jane, working her way into my calf, finding the points where the muscle attaches to the bone, working the points, encouraging the muscle to release, to let go.

"So she jumps on him," I say. "Throws herself at him. They roll down the stairs and she starts punching him. 'Throttling him,' were her words, 'beating the shit out of him.' She could do it. She's skinny, but she's tall. She's got muscle on her. Finally, they pulled her off him. She picked up her bag and went on her way. To her shoot."

"What was he," says Jane. "A lawyer or something?"

Patsy now taunting me, telling me that she may learn to love again, but I don't believe her. How can I?

"People just hate Trix," I say, "for what she has. They hate her because they can't be her, I guess. It's the Africa in her, some kind of exotic aura. They think she's a movie star or something."

"Pam has it, too," says Jane. "Whatever it is. Maybe it is an African thing, a primal thing."

"Pam has," I say, "the mirror image of it. People love it in Pam. They hate it in Trix. The evil twin."

Jane rubs more lotion into her hands and pushes upward on the top of my thigh, a friendly hello-how-are-you-today? survey of my quadriceps.

"That's why you married Pam and not Trix," says Jane.

A new voice singing, a whining voice, as if through the walls, a hint of steel guitar, as Hank Williams tells me my cheating heart will make me weep, make me cry when I try to sleep.

"I didn't know Trix," I say, "when I married Pam. But, yes, I guess you're right. That's why I did. Pam is actually probably more exotic than Trix, more of a classical movie star type, more Leslie Caron and Sophia Loren, less Greta Garbo, less Madonna, less bad girl. But they all appeal to me, they always have, these foreign women. I am attracted to them, to the exotic, to the 'other' as the anthropologists say. I don't know why, I'm a pretty unexotic kind of guy when you get down to it. I mean, look at me."

"I do," she says, "all the time."

"And?"

"You're right," she says. "You're a pretty unexotic kind of guy."

The disembodied singing voice, Hank in an original recording, still singing about tears, how they remind him of the falling rain.

"I'm self-deprecating," I say. "Self-defecating, too."

"Most people are," says Jane. "You might not be, though."

"When you stop being self-defecating," I say, "they put you in a home."

She's into my hamstrings now, on the inside of my leg, working them hard, searching for trigger points, the circuit breakers, finding one, digging her fingers in. The pain starts to come.

"Tight," says Jane. "Your hamstrings are really tight again. Have you been doing your stretches?"

My cheating heart. How does Hank know? How does he know about me?

"Rigor mortis," I say, "setting in. Habeas corpus. Incognito. In flagrante delicto. Latin phrases. Words to hide behind. Do you have to press so hard?"

"Sorry," she says, but the pressure remains and the pain radiates.

"Writers hate Latin words," I say. "Anglo-Saxon words have more punch. Think of the difference between fuck and fornicate."

"There is," she says, "a difference?"

"There is," I say, "semiotically speaking."

She moves into my groin, reaching down to the bottom of the pelvis, under my genitals, finding another point of attachment. The agony is hot this time, and sudden. I sink into a frozen moment of pain.

"Did I ever tell you," I say, "about the time I met Wilfred Brimley?"

"The one who looks like a walrus," she says. "The Quaker Oats guy."

"That's him," I say. "Mr. Grandpops."

"You probably did," she says. "But tell me again. I'll see if you tell it the same as you did last time."

"Does that matter?"

"Not really," she says. "Just as long as it's funny."

"Diverting."

"Yes."

"Something to take you out of yourself for a moment," I say. "Transport you to a world of glamour—"

"Just tell the story," she says. "Okay? Tell me about Wilfred."

"It was in Little Rock," I say. "Mary Steenbergen had just finished shooting a movie about her father's life. Daddy worked for the railroad. Mary played her mother—her own mother, if you can believe it—and Wilfred played her father, some crusty gruff old switchman with the traditional heart of gold but put upon, you know, by the evil forces of capital, this time railroad moguls in Chicago or someplace. Just imagine that conceit: getting some Hollywood studio to give you money to make an homage to mom and dad with cliched robber barons as the bad guys. How many times have you seen that before?"

"Couple," she says, her thumbs now buried deep into my flesh, almost reaching the pelvic bone. The pain is white. I emit a small cry. She relaxes a bit.

"Anyhow," I say, "there was a wrap party and somehow I was invited. A really bad band and equally bad Mexican food. I snuck out the back door and there was Wilfred Brimley leaning against the fender of a pickup truck. He had a beer in his hand and a giant cowboy hat on his head. He couldn't have been five two. His stomach stuck out a mile. His moustache was covered in beer foam and salsa. He looked at me and he said, 'Fucking cunt of a bitching whore.' I said something like, 'Pardon me?' and he said, 'I said fucking whore of a cunting bitch.' I asked him if he was talking about a singular human being, maybe a woman I might know, maybe a famous female movie star, some bit of gossip I might pass along to the *National Enquirer* or something. 'I am talking about,' he said, 'my muse.' His eyes locked onto me. 'My muse!' Then he said, 'Fucking cunt that she is.'"

"Well," says Jane. "Sure makes me want to buy his oatmeal."

"I know," I say. "Makes me want to go to law school."

"Don't," says Jane, "say that."

Her hands are deep into my lower abdomen now, probing what seems to be my bladder, trying to find muscles under organs. Pain shoots down into my testicles.

"What the hell," I say, "are you doing down there?"

"Trigger points," she says, "for all those little muscles in your groin, the ones that are so tight they could be said to define atrophy."

Another shooting pain.

"Jesus Christ," I say.

"Getting a little referral, are we," she says.

"We," I say, "are."

"Good," she says. "At least your nervous system is working. Which is more than I can say for most of your muscles. Rocks aren't this hard."

She moves into my stomach and feeling begins to return.

"Watch out," I say, "for my spleen. Spleens rupture you know."

"Yours," she says, "vents. Constantly."

"Cute," I say. "Clever."

"I have never," says Jane, "known anybody as tight as you. So tense all over. The only way you can effectively start dealing with it is the stretching. You've got to do those stretches or you're going to end up like hard taffy in cold water."

"Brittle," I say.

"Brittle," she says, "is too kind a word."

"Peanut brittle."

"Stress," she says. "All though your body."

"The corporeal manifestation of it," I say. "Of peanut brittle."

"Stop it," she says.

"Chuck," I say, "my friend Chuck in LA, the guy who manages variety acts, was telling me about a new one he found. A little girl, maybe ten or eleven, who weighs eighty pounds. Her gimmick is that nobody can lift her off the ground if she doesn't want them to. I mean, two hundred fifty pound linebackers can't make her budge, not if she doesn't want to. He says it's the most amazing thing he's ever seen. Says he has no idea how she does it."

"You know lots of bizarre people," says Jane. "You have a very strange life, these memories, these people calling you up all the time."

"I know," I say. "I run, but I can't hide."

"You're obsessed," she says, "with clichés."

"I am obsessed," I say, "with clichés, among other things. With myself, among other things."

Her hands clasp firmly on either side of my head and slowly, confidently pull it back, away from my shoulders and spine. Her fingers, strong and sure, reach into the back of my neck, separating and stretching out the muscles there. I feel them lengthen. I feel blood flowing.

"I worry about you," she says.

"I worry about me, too," I say.

She uses two fingers on each hand to gently rub my temples, employing just the right touch, releasing the pressure around my eyes. Tension seeps away.

"But I don't worry about you," I say. "You love what you do. You like people, you're happy in your work, happy in your life."

"I know," she says. "I am."

"I used to be that way."

Patsy is back, remembering our faded love. With every heart beat, she remembers . . .

"Maybe," I say, "I could be that way again."

She's grabbing my hair in small clumps, twisting it, working her way around my head, releasing the muscles in my scalp. My brain seems to move beyond the confines of my skull, to spread out and bask.

"But you know," she says, "secretly, deep down inside, what I really want to be is—"

"Please," I say, "don't tell me."

"What I'd like to be," she says, "is a TV weatherman."

I say, "I really didn't want to hear that."

"Poor you," she says.

"Poor you, too," I say.

"I just love watching the jet stream," she says. "Figuring out where it'll be tomorrow. Me and the jet stream on TV, with mamma and all the kids watching us . . . "

"I feel," I say, "like a recovering alcoholic trapped in a liquor store and all I do all day long, all I can do, what I am forced to do, is walk around and listen to the labels on the bottles read themselves to me."

"That," she says, "is profound."

"Shut," I say, "up."

"That," she says, "makes absolutely no sense whatsoever."

"Like my life," I say. "Like my head talking . . . Unable to stop . . . Not wanting to . . . Rambling, like a rose or something . . . "

"Sssshhh . . . " she whispers.

She gives my ears a gentle twist and then she covers my eyes with her dry, warm hands. I feel the pulse in her fingers, in my forehead.

Language . . . should take the form of dialogue . . . in dialogue language maintains the distance between the two; "their commerce," as Levinas puts it, "is ethical." Dialogism allows for "the radical separation, the strangeness of the interlocutors, the revelation of the other to me." The structure of dialogue, moreover, disallows the taking up of any position beyond the interlocutors from which they can be integrated into a larger totality. The relation between them, therefore, is not oppositional, nor limitrophe, but one of alterity.

—Robert Young, *White Mythologies: Writing History and the West*

I have wondered time and again about my reading myself as I feel he reads me and my false encounter with the other in me whose non-being/being he claims to have captured, solidified, and pinned to a butterfly board. Like any common living thing, I fear and reprove classification and the death it entails, and I will not allow its clutches to lock down on me, although I realize I can never lure myself into simply escaping it. The difference, as I sense it, is: naming, like a cast of the die, is just one step toward unnaming, a tool to render visible what he has carefully kept invisible in his manipulative blindness.

—Trinh Minh-ha, *Woman, Native, Other*

8

Wonder Never Seizes

A passion named wonder...Wonder never seizes, never possesses the other as its object. It is in the ability to see, hear, and touch, to go toward things as though always for the first time. The encounter is one that surprises in its unexpected, if not entirely unknown character.

—Trinh Minh-ha, *The Moon Waxes Red*

For the cultural critic must attempt to fully realize, and take responsibility for, the unspoken, unrepresented pasts that haunt our historical present.

—Homi Bhabha, *The Location of Culture*

"Are you writing this down?" asks Trix.

"Some of it," I say. "The occasional line or phrase."

I hear her lighting one of her small cigars, the badly rolled black Pockets that Dieter sends her from Munich. Trix on the other end of the telephone line, a thousand miles away, in New York City.

I envision her sitting on the love seat in front of the window, the large sheet of clear plastic still taped to the frame against the cold, distorting the gaseous lights outside. The large red curtains, so brilliant in the sun, now heavy and muted, blood black in the dead of night.

"Good," she says. "I want you to write me again. I want you to make me famous. God knows I'm never going to make it by myself."

"You are famous," I say. "In certain circles."

"Aach, yah," she says, in that South African accent of hers, betraying Afrikaner roots, summers on a farm in the Orange Free State, a born member of the white tribe.

"Aach, yah is right," I say.

"Fucking famous maybe," she says, "famous for fucking." She laughs.

"Listen to me," she says. "Just listen to me."

I write down "fucking famous...famous for fucking" on a yellow legal pad next to the keyboard. Then I write "Orange Free State." With my right hand, I open a computer file.

Words on the screen:

draft

Look at Us Now: Celebrity and the Third Space[1]

Homi Bhabha's Third Space, Giorgio Agamben's Coming Community, Trinh Minh-ha's Third Scenario—we attempt to take these concepts, among others, and meld them into a working scenario of celebrity in postmodern times.

For Bhabha, Trinh and Agamben the redemptive strategies/ spaces of our times occur primarily in liminal spaces—unstable spaces in between, on the threshold, spaces that encompass...

"You have a way with words," I say to Trix.

"I know," she says. "Sometimes I amaze myself."

"Do you want to see some pictures?" asks Trix.

I am in her apartment for the first time, a crooked place above a diner in Long Island City, one long subway stop from Grand Central, just across the East River, behind and under the large Pepsi sign that UN bureaucrats gaze at through blue-green-tinted panes. Long Island City, an Italian Greek enclave seven minutes on the 7 train from the hurly burly, lost in the 1950s, languishing in a time warp of short decaying buildings and badly angled streets.

Trix's rooms seem to have no corners, Van Gogh rooms where round things always roll, never coming to rest.

The first picture is black and white, the face of an extremely old black woman, taken in blinding sunlight, a thinning tangle of white hair bleeding into the white sky that surrounds her. Her eyes are gray and filled with spots, the irises indistinguishable from the whites, the pupils so small that I cannot locate them. Her skin is heavily lined, deep crevices that wind their way across her forehead and down her cheeks into her neck, empty rivers worn smooth, no doubt unexpectedly soft to the touch, not yet ready to crumble. An unbothered upside-down fly, its wings limp and transparent, clings to her chin.

"I took that on my grandmother's farm in the karoo near Buffelsklip," says Trix. *She sits on an orange crate across from me, leaning forward, her back straight and long. Her knees are touching mine.*

"And the woman?"

"Aach," says Trix, "she's always been there, since I was a child. Everybody is related to her in some way. Great face, huh?"

"Nice photograph."

"I took it just before Christmas," she says. "Maybe next year I'll make Christmas cards out of it."

Trix places another one on top of the old woman.

"And this," she says, "is me."

And it is, completely naked, sitting on the same uncomfortable green metal garden bench where I now find myself perched. Her arms hang long and thin along her sides, her whole body thin, bones showing, sticking out, breasts small and high as if moved out of the way to reveal knobbed ribs above the sunken cavity of her stomach above almost fleshless hips and legs, starkly white in the light of a single flash, a motionless concentration camp body. And, instead of a face, a streak of shiny red hair, long and alive like a cracking whip, a taunting highlit blur moving too fast for the fastest shutter.

Trix laughs.

"Funny, huh?" she says.

"Nice," I say, "nicely done."

Trix, the tall thin South African model, always covered from head to toe in black or green, so beautiful as to be intimidating on the streets of New York, yet also so shy, always refusing to go to the pool because she doesn't like how she looks in a swimming costume. Trix, now naked before me.

> *She laughs again.*
> *"I'm shocking you," she says.*
> *"No . . . "*
> *"I took it myself," she says, "with the timer. Don't you just love it?"*

"You are amazement personified," I say. "Did you vote today?"

"I did," she said. "It was a madhouse, hundreds of people, quite exciting. I knew there were a lot of South Africans in New York, but Jesus, it looked like New Year's Day at Camps Bay . . . "

"And who'd you vote for?"

"The ANC, of course," she says, pronouncing it as a word, "anck," not spelling out the letters like they do on television.

"The anck?" I say, repeating. "You call them the anck?"

"Everybody does," she says. "Like the sound a pig makes."

"Pigs," I say, "say oink, not anck."

"That's what I said," she says. "Anck. The pig sound. The African National Congress."

"You're calling Nelson Mandela a pig?"

"Aach, man, no," she says. "It's just a sound, faster to say than A-N-C."

"Fewer syllables," I say.

"Fewer," she says. "Although I did vote for the Nationals in the Western Cape. They're sure to win there, not enough ancks in the Western Cape."

I write down, "ANC = anck . . . like ankle . . . or knee or foot . . . a pig sound . . . "

I page down on the computer screen:

. . . Agamben's "perfect exteriority," that transcend dialectics of recognition, spaces with new futures, different temporalities, histories, and terminologies, spaces that offer the hope of fresh political possibilities, that constantly interrogate the taken-for-granted categories of race, gender, class, etc.

"Remember," says Trix, "when Jake and I were on that plane from Joburg to Cape Town and Pik Botha was sitting next to us and he got so drunk that he cried?"

"Because he could see it coming?"

"That's right," says Trix. "Because he knew it would happen while he was in power, because he knew he would help it happen. 'On our watch' was how he put it. Like he was fucking Churchill or something. That was shortly after P. K.'s stroke. Or maybe shortly before. I can't remember."

"Pik Botha fucked Churchill?"

"Maybe," says Trix. "If not, he certainly will in the movie version. Big time."

"Listen," I say, "to what Rey Chow says. I'm putting her in this paper I'm working on ... "

"You're going to read to me again?" she says. "You love to read to me, don't you?"

"Consider yourself one of the privileged few," I say. "So, Rey Chow says, 'It is only through thinking of the other as sharing our time and speaking to us at the moment of writing that we can find an alternative to allochronism—' Allochronism is a nation-centered theory of culture. '—The position of the feminized, ethnicized spectator, as image as well as gaze, object of ethnography as well as subject in cultural transformations, is a position for which coevalness is inevitable'" (Chow 1991, p. 33).

"I'll buy into that," says Trix. "We can never have too much coevalness."

"I thought you liked it when I read to you," I say.

"I do," says Trix. "Most of all when you are reading me something you wrote about me, about how you're going to make me famous."

"Indulge me," I say.

"Indulge me," she says. "Here's something you can write down and read back to me next month, before you send it to *The New Yorker* or give it to some professor."

"You've had an adventure," I say. "Why'd you wait so long to tell me?"

"Teasing you," she says. "Waiting for you to ask. Remember the diner, the one downstairs?"

*   *   *

The door is covered with fading hand-lettered signs announcing hours and bingo games long over. I have just come up from the subway into Long Island City, into the smell of ramshackle exhaust, of unleaded fuels and burning olive oil. I am in a place I've never been before and the feeling of a stranger, alone, lost, afraid, comes over me. This is not the New York of Little Italy, not the mean streets of the Lower East Side. This is a foreign land, a backwater, a forgotten and sleepy place where the danger flows in palpable undercurrents. I force myself to walk through the door marked "Diner" into a narrow room with a stooled counter running down the center. Two swarthy men in greasy aprons look up from frying eggs to watch me enter. A large woman in fading polyester hunches over a cup of coffee at the end of counter. She turns to stare at me. Smoke from her cigarette drifts languidly toward a loud, dusty exhaust fan.

"Nate!"

It is Trix's voice. She sits alone in a red plastic booth. I slide in across from her.

"You found it okay?" says Trix.

"Easy," I say. "You give good directions."

"Pete," she says to one of the counter men, "bring my friend a glass of orange juice."

Pete nods and says, "Sure, Trix."

"It's good here," she says. "Greeks always squeeze good orange juice."

She already has a glass full in front of her on the formica table-top, a yellow-tinted plastic glass, the kind of plastic you can taste. She reaches up into her piled-high auburn hair and pulls out a small long-handled silver spoon. It looks Victorian, delicate. With it she shovels a large amount of blue-green algae from a dark brown bottle into the juice and stirs. Instantly, as if through the magic of alchemy, the orange liquid turns black-green. She lifts the glass to her lips and drinks it down, chugging it, as if it were muddied green beer in Chicago on St. Patrick's Day. She puts the glass down and smiles at me. Her teeth are green.

"Your teeth are green," I say.

"Like my eyes," she says.

And she laughs.

"Like your soul," I say.

"Like Africa."

"Like money."

"Like my hard hard petrifying heart," she says, and she laughs again.

Without a word, Pete puts a glass of orange juice in front of me, the plastic touching the formica with a certain hollow indifference.

"So," she says, "this is my diner. Isn't it everything I told you it was? Don't you just love it?"

I am drawing interlocking triangles on the yellow pad. New words, with the help of my index finger, have inched their way onto the computer screen:

Bhabha's Third Space is a possibility opened up only to those living in the colonized position; that is, the Third Space is a way in which the subordinate undoes and unsettles the dialectic of the colonizer. Agamben's Coming Community is born in oscillation, moving between communion and disaggregation, a community completely without presuppositions. Trinh Minh-ha's assault on binarisms finds the challenge in the hyphen itself, "the realm in-between, where predetermined rules cannot fully apply" (p. 157).

"How could I forget the diner," I say. "I can still smell it."

I write "diner" on the pad, followed by "liminal space...between here and here..." I write "Trix" with lots of Xs overlapping.

"When was it?" says Trix. "Last Thursday night I think. I was in there late with Janine, having some coffee. Around midnight these five guys walked in. Four of them were real heavy dudes, lots of black leather covered in lightning bolts and skulls and things. Biker types. The real thing, not drugstore. Short short hair, earrings, big boots, brass knuckles, big guys, young, tough. The fifth guy was short and old, bags under his eyes, carrying a beat-up old briefcase. They all crammed into a booth. I mean, guys like this don't come into my diner."

"Sort of out of place," I say. "Between here and here, out of gas, out of luck."

"No, not like that," says Trix. "They were having a business meeting of some kind. They were writing on napkins. One of the guys was, well, you know, kind of cute, tall and cute. I pointed him out to Janine and she agreed. Once he caught me staring at him and I said, 'Nice jacket,' something dumb like that. He smiled, but didn't say anything. Janine kept nudging me, telling me to go over and introduce myself, say something to him, but I didn't. I mean, I don't do stuff like that. You know that, I don't."

"I know," I say. "Guys come up to you."

"All the time, the fuckers," says Trix. "Anyhow, after a while Janine and I left and went up to my place—it's right upstairs, you know . . . "

"I've been there," I say. "I know."

"So, it was about half an hour later and Janine and I were drinking some wine and she kept telling me that I should have said something to him, given him my phone number. She was kind of goading me, but I liked it, I didn't care. After a while—and remember I've never ever done anything like this before—after a while I picked up the phone and called the diner. Pete answered and I asked him if those guys were still there and he said yeah they were. I described the cute one to him and Pete said did I want to talk to him and I said yes I did, so he called him over to the phone. He picked it up and—now this was really embarrassing, but what can I say?—he said hello in some foreign language and I said, 'I'm sorry I don't speak Italian,' and he said, in English, 'it's not Italian, it's Portuguese.' I wanted to say it's all Greek to me, but I didn't, didn't want to be too flip, I just told him that I was the girl who liked his jacket and I said I thought he was cute and if he wanted he could give me a call sometime . . . "

"So you gave him your number? This guy you've never met? In New York? You did that?"

"I did," says Trix. "Like Mae West would have done."

"Jesus, Trix," I say.

"Jesus," says Trix, "is right."

I write on the pad, "Holly Golightly . . . New York in the '50s, Truman Capote . . ." then I draw a big X through it, like Derrida would do.

"So then what happened?"

"Nothing. He didn't say anything and I hung up. About an hour later the doorbell rang and he was there."

"And you let him in."

"I did. He came up and had some wine with Janine and me. Turned out he's Brazilian, kind of shy, quiet, in this band with the other guys in the diner. They rehearse in an old warehouse over by the river. The old guy's their manager. He's English, used to manage the Sex Pistols or something."

"The Sex Pistols?" I say. "Couldn't he have said something more au currant, like Nirvana maybe? He actually said the Sex Pistols?"

"It's New York," says Trix. "And he said the Sex Pistols. How was I to know what was true? How do I know anything's true? He could have been an alien. He could have been an axe murderer or something. He could be anything. He could even, possibly, be something close to what he says he is. I mean, I could be an axe murderess, too. How would he know? How would anybody know? Until I hauled out the axe or something."

"You could be an axe murderess," I say. "I know some people who think you are."

"Stop it," says Trix. "I don't even own an axe. A chain saw, yes, but not an axe. Be kind, now, or I'll stop."

"I'm always kind," I say. "You know that. You know me."

"I'm telling you this because you asked."

"I did?"

"You always do," she says. "Sometimes not outright, but you always ask. Otherwise, why would I bother?"

"Because you think I'll write it all down and make you famous?"

"Because you listen," she says. "Because I love telling you things. Because my life's like a subway stop."

"Like a subway stop?"

"So many people passing through," she says. "I have to tell somebody just to keep track."

"And you tell me."

"I can't stop," she says. "Doing stuff and telling you about it."

"You the addict," I say. "Me the drug."

"I know," she says. "There's a party in my head and you're always invited, no cover charge."

"Lucky me," I say. "So, tell me more. Please."

"Well," she says, "after a while Janine left and we sat there, staring at each other and I thought, my God, what a handsome devil, shy, with a nervous smile, his hand shaking. At times, he was shaking all over, maybe more scared than I was. I mean, he was like a little boy. So, we smoked a joint."

I page down on the computer to the next screen:

We see these philosophers (although their languages differ) privileging performativity as the major consciousness in/of the alternative spaces they seek to reveal—the inbetweenness and thresholdness of the flow of human life in culture is enacted through performativity. They stress the many modes/levels of being/experience that are performed: people, living and moving in culture, metaphorically seeing and trying to read themselves and others in signifying actions, strategies, costumes, identities. In his descriptions of these spaces, Bhabha notes their ambiguity and temporary natures, but nevertheless points to the empowerment that comes from residing in and about these communities, from performing in the Third Space.

I move the cursor up the screen and replace the word "philosophers" with "writers." I run the spell checker on the paragraph and find that "performativity," "inbetweenness," and "thresholdness" don't exist. I leave them in anyway.

"He's a rock star, then, this guy?" I say. "Does he have a name? Have you learned it by this time?"

"Yes," says Trix, "I have. It's Supla. His name is Supla..."

"Can you spell that?"

"S-U-P-L-A."

I write it down.

"That's a Brazilian name?" I say.

"How would I know?" says Trix. "It's his name. I know that for sure; I saw it sewn into his underpants."

She laughs. I hear her lighting another cigar, no doubt with the old Zippo lighter she keeps in a Gucci shoe box next to her bed.

"You know what Toni Morrison says about names, what Beloved, one of her women characters, says?"

"No."

"She says, 'I want you to touch me on my inside part and call me my name.' It's about a desire for identity, a desperate cry."

"It's sad," says Trix. "I know what she means. I want that too, sometimes."

"Even from a rock star?" I say.

"Fuck you," says Trix.

"I love it when you say that," I say. "When I can make you say that."

"And yes, even from a rock star," says Trix. "He is a rock star, you know. At least in Brazil. He also plays polo and acoustic guitar and he's a boxer, too. His father is a politician of some kind, a state senator or something, and his mother is a psychologist. He says she is the Dr. Ruth of Brazil."

I write down "Dr. Ruth of Brazil...underpants" and I underline "pants" and write next to it, "not underwear..." And then I write "See Homi Bhabha on Toni Morrison and Nadine Gordimer..."

"So," I say. "How old is Supla?"

"Two years younger than me," says Trix. "He's twenty-eight, a nice age for a boy."

"And his astrological sign?"

"Aach, man!" says Trix.

"Okay," I say. "Okay..."

"So," says Trix, "I told Supla that I never did this on the first joint..."

"This?"

"And that. You know, fuck. It was kind of a joke, because we hadn't done it yet and it didn't look like we would. He laughed. We sat there talking for another hour or so, it was now like four in the morning or something and we were both so so tired we had no idea what we were saying. So I suggested that we take a bath."

"A bath?" I say.

"Yes."

"In your tub?"

"In my tub."

"Okay," I say, "so where is this famous bathtub?"

"I've been saving it for last," says Trix. We are in her kitchen. There is no stove, no refrigerator, no hot plate. Just an old toaster oven covered with dust and a rust-colored sink with a broken pizza box in it.

"This way . . ."

We walk halfway down an uneven windowless corridor. On one wall there is a heavy green curtain. She pulls it back.

"And this," she says, "is my bathroom."

It is tiny, not even a room, more like a shallow cave hacked out of the wall. There is a toilet and a large sink, that is all. I look at the sink. It is a shiny silver stainless steel restaurant sink, three feet square, sitting a few inches off the concrete floor on bricks.

"That's your bathtub?"

"Yes," says Trix. "Isn't it magnificent?"

"It's a sink," I say.

"I know," she says. "Well, let's say it was a sink. Now it's a bathtub. My bathtub. Where I live."

On a small shelf to the side of the sink and on the floor around it are dozens of half-melted green candles and green bottles with charred incense sticks in them. On the back of the toilet are open perfume bottles, most filled with greenish liquid, and in a box between the toilet and the sink are several bottles of photo-finishing chemicals.

"I put it in myself," says Trix. "I hammered out the door frame so I could get it in and then I poured that concrete slab and I hung the curtain so I can also use it as a darkroom. I did all the plumbing myself, too."

"Isn't it a little cramped?" I say. "I mean, you must be six feet tall . . ."

"Five ten and a half," she says. "And no, it's not cramped, it's perfect. I'm a lot more flexible than you'd think. Here, look."

And she climbs into the tub and sits there, her knees up either side of her face, smiling, content.

"I can even do this," she says and she pulls one leg up behind her head, effortlessly, naturally.

"I spend hours in here," she says. "It's my favorite place in the whole world."

"A three-foot-by-three-foot-by-three-foot stainless steel box?"

"Exactly," says Trix. "I bring my phone and my bottle of champagne and I'm in heaven."

She puts her leg down, hugs her knees and laughs.

"I know you think I'm crazy," she says.

"Well..." I say.

"Come on," she says, "take my picture. Memorialize me and my bathtub."

I pull my Olympus Stylus from my pocket and snap off several frames.

I write down "memorialize me and my bathtub..." and "poses like a model, suddenly professional, first smiling, then not...," then I cross it all out and circle the words "memorialize me."

"Must have been a tight fit," I say.

"It was," says Trix. "He's like six-four or something. I've never known a guy that tall. It's nice, nice having someone tall, someone who is really taller than me. It's a cliché, I know, but it's nice, bending my neck that way."

"He's as flexible as you, then?"

"And gorgeous, too," she says. "All rippling muscle and smooth smooth skin. It was a perfect fit in my tub, two peas in a pod."

"One South African, one Brazilian."

"Exactly," says Trix.

"One a famous photographer, the other a famous rock star, meeting by chance in Long Island City," I say. "A place in between."

"Exactly exactly," says Trix. "Exactly."

On the computer screen:

In our essay, we take the concept of celebrity (and its pursuit) in postmodernity—celebrity generally referring to fame, achieved recognition, and other qualities associated with movie stars, sport heroes, Hollywood, the tabloids, being on/in television, in the movies, in the public eye, etc.—and explore such celebrity as one working example of a Third Space or Coming Community.

"Jesus, Trix," I say. "You are something."

"I know," she says. "Did I tell you that the name of his band is Mad Parade? It's heavy, heavy metal, high energy, and Supla, gentle Supla, writes all the songs."

"No, you didn't tell me," I say. "So, it's not world beat."

"God, no," says Trix.

"You won't find Willie Nelson rerecording Supla songs in about ten years, then?"

"I don't think so," says Trix. "For that kind of thing, for heavy metal, it's good. I mean, I wouldn't buy it, but I don't mind listening to it."

"And there's nothing Brazilian about it?"

"Nothing," she says. "Except him. He's Brazilian. What comes out of his mouth is Ozzie Osborne, a better Ozzie Osborne than Ozzie Osborne. Anyhow, do you want to hear the rest of what happened or not?"

"I do," I say.

"Well," says Trix, "we still hadn't actually done it. I mean, we'd played around and stuff, but we hadn't actually fucked. You know how you are when you get so tired your eyes start swimming and things that aren't supposed move start moving and won't stop? Well, we were that tired. Somehow, we got from the tub to the bed and fell fast asleep. I woke up about eight, he was still sleeping, still there, and I ran into Beto's room—"

"Who?" I say.

"Beto," says Trix, "my new roommate, the Venezuelan gay guy. You didn't meet him?"

"No," I say.

"He's sweet," says Trix. "I woke him up and said that I had this beautiful beautiful man in my bed and I didn't know what to do. And he said, 'Trix, Trix, go for it! My God, Trix, don't think about it, go for it!' And he gave me some really expensive condoms. So, I went for it."

Trix giggles.

I write down: "Beto ... Venezuela ... condoms ... "

"And?" I say.

"And," she says, "it was really great. Jesus, it was great. He's got this incredible body, thin and strong with lots of muscle, really well defined, soft and hard at the same time. It was fantastic. He didn't leave till close to noon. I just couldn't get enough of him. His stomach is like a riddle of muscles that I can ride like a wave."

"What did you say?"

She laughs.

"I said," she says, "his stomach is like a riddle of muscles I can ride like a wave."

I write that down, word for word.

"I thought that's what you said," I say. "I like 'riddle of muscle,' the idea it evokes."

"Beto got a look at him and he said to me, 'My God, Trix, beautiful face, big legs, big ass, perfect, congratulations!'"

I am writing fast now.

"You do a wonderful Spanish accent," I say.

"I know," says Trix, "I've been practicing."

"And Supla," I say, "how'd he like it? How's he like you, do you think?"

"I don't know," says Trix. "What's more important is how much I liked it. He's like a combination of a wild cat and a pussy cat, a wild dog and a tame dog. I could show him what I liked and he'd do it like I wanted, only better. It was fantastic."

"So you sort of used him," I say. "Exploited him."

"I'm a cultivator, not an exploiter," says Trix. "I'm a gardener."

I write down "cultivator, not exploiter, gardener ... chauncey gardener ... secret garden of delights ... rain forest ... the garden route, joburg–cape town ... "

"That's nice," I say.

And I write, "cultivate = culturate ... enculturate ... "

"And he's so big," she says, dragging on a cigar, "what's the phrase? ... so well endowed."

"He is?"

"Gigantic," she says. "Beto says all Brazilians are big. It's a national characteristic. And Beto should know."

"And it makes a difference?"

"Yeah," she says, "it does. I know people say it doesn't, I used to think it didn't, but yeah, it does, it makes a big difference."

"And it's an essential Brazilian characteristic."

"It could grow to become essential, yes," says Trix. "I could become addicted to big dicks."

I write down, "essentialist ... Brazil ... well endowed ... "

"Just listen to me," says Trix. "Listen to how I am talking."

"I know," I say. "And you've never done this before."

"I haven't," she says. "It's the first time. Honest to God. I have never picked up anybody before, ever. Never slept with anyone on the first date, ever. Never."

She laughs.

"Funny, huh?" she says. "With a Brazilian. With a rock star."

"Strange."

"You know," she says. "I think he's used to having groupies, I mean he must, being a singer and all. So, I was thinking about that, and I said to him at one point, 'I'm not your groupie, I'm no one's groupie, I'm my own groupie.' "

"And?" I say.

"He laughed," she said. "He thought it was funny, what I said. And then I laughed. He's very funny, you know. Very sweet and innocent in his own way, with that kind of easy Latin self-confidence, making a joke of it. Nonthreatening when he wants to be, in spite of all the leather and shit."

I page down on the computer screen:

Celebrity appears to meet some of the criteria of Bhabha's Third Space: in celebrity, contemporary discourses are mimicked, parodied, erased; in celebrity, where performativity is truly privileged, hegemony can be contested; in celebrity, we may find a kind of "perfect exteriority." Certainly, (what passes for) the masses recognize celebrity as a Third Space, one of the few redeeming strategic positions open to them in a postmodern world. That is why, in part, everyone everywhere seems to be questing after the salvation promised by Warhol—the infamous 15 minutes of fame.

I write down: "performativity ... supla performing ... "

"And he just left?" I say.

"He had a meeting or something, he had some place to go," she says. "And I had work to do. He said he'd call or maybe stop by. A great story, huh?"

"Great."

"You'll write it, then?" she says.

"You should write it," I say.

"Aach," says Trix, "how can I? I'm living it."

With the down arrow key, I bring up the next paragraph:

We discuss within our work—which itself is constructed as performative—whether celebrity is institutionalized liminality, whether celebrity can be theoretically constructed/deconstructed as a Third Space. Finally, we look at how we celebrate ourselves, as we explore the space(s) in which we find ourselves to see if we indeed are crying for attention from a place of (in)difference, somewhere in between.

We are walking down Vernon Boulevard in Long Island City on Saturday afternoon toward the blue bridge over the rusted railroad spur, past padlocked Italian social clubs, dust-covered silver cups forgotten in their delicately arranged window displays, nobody on the street but us and an occasional car, a taxi cab or two with the blotched yellow skin of a punch-drunk prizefighter.

Trix, her face white and her hair approaching the color of African mahogany in the coldly angled winter sunlight, is dressed in high-fashion black—black boots with raised heels and soles, a long, fitted black skirt severely slit to reveal black tights, a jacket too thin for the cold, colored a dark dark green, like the black-green of the lowest leaf in the thickest corner of a Brazilian rain forest.

She stoops to pick up a twisted piece of metal about the size of a crowbar, a tangle of rusting steel cut in no particular shape, a seeming remnant from a disgruntled CNC machine, probably fallen from the bed of a passing junk truck, jarred loose by an angry pothole.

"I like this," she says. "What do you think?"

"It looks kind of heavy," I say. "Kind of vicious."

"I can use it in my welding class," she says. "It can be a part of what I'm making, my project, my postatomic rose."

"Welding class?"

"I'm making this gnarly, twisted rose," she says. "It's as tall as I am, with a five-foot stem. Mostly it's ragged gunmetal gray, but with

streaks of silver in it, really rough. It's going to be a lovely piece, weighs a ton."

"Made from scrap metal you found on the street?"

"Yes," she says. "On the streets of Long Island City and in the scrap heaps behind the abandoned factories over there, toward the river."

"A scavenger."

"Pepe gave me a large metal key and a small metal heart," she says. "They're a part of it, too. I made thorns out of them."

Trix laughs.

"Pepe?"

"Pepe's Spanish or Mexican or something," she says. "Just a friend, an Upper West Side boy from south of the border, teaches the tango or something. Sweet Pepe, like a sweet red bell pepper, my sweet Pepe."

"Jesus, Trix."

"I know," she says, "but I can't help it."

We pass a garage with an open door. Inside are half a dozen yellow cabs in various stages of undress, dirty men exploring their gritty bowels with gleaming socket wrenches. A knot of men stumbles out into the street behind us and we turn to look. Cab drivers, mostly Indian, some Sikhs in turbans who are smoking brown cigarettes. They look after us for a second, then huddle around a lamppost and speak words to each other in a language I can neither understand nor identify.

Trix slips the piece of twisted metal into her large black bag.

"Stupid fuckers," she says. "The taxi companies all have garages along here because it's so close to town. The drivers are always hanging out, leering, like they were back in Bangladesh or someplace. You'd think they never saw a white woman before, never saw a fucking movie."

We round a corner and walk down a broad street toward the river, past the loading docks for the Pepsi bottling plant, the one with the large sign that so dominates the view from the United Nations. A few women, mostly young, black, and giggling loudly, drift away from the large doors and make their way up toward Vernon Avenue. Their voices hush as they pass us.

At the water's edge, I absorb the view. Manhattan's classic skyline shimmers before me, a picture postcard.

"Look at that," I say.

I point directly across the river to a street that runs toward us, an open space between the tall buildings, a space that bisects the island, a space of white sky for as far as the eye can see, starting at ground level and extending heavenward, separating the tall buildings, cutting their jagged flow in half.

"Strange," says Trix. "I never noticed that before."

"I wonder what street it could be," I say. "Maybe Forty-Second Street."

"Maybe," says Trix, looking down the street, her gaze filling the space. "Somebody cut Manhattan in half and left a little space in between. It's lovely."

"Forty-Second Street," I say. "Busby Berkeley's street."

"I'm going to put my postatomic rose on wheels," says Trix, "so I can roll it around my apartment. I want it to feel at home all over my place, to be wherever I am, to go wherever it wants to go. The rose part is going to be a candle holder."

"A six-foot-tall candle holder?"

"For a big fat green candle," says Trix. "One that will shine a little light on me."

I merge another file into my document, a few rough paragraphs. The words on the screen read:

Until this century, mass populations in human communities had little opportunity for expressing imaginative impulses in large mediatized spaces such as those that now abound in television, film, sport arenas, amphitheaters. In pre and early modernity, fantasies for common folk were restricted to rituals, song, dance, story-telling, fairs, plastic arts—all localized narratives. Only nobility, gentry, the elite, had the resources to flesh out creations in the shape of things like pageants, theater, pamphlets, distinctive dwellings, athletic pursuits, gardens, and other fanciful structures. However problematic it is to construct events out of time periods, or even to label a time period as a construct, we must still notice, within the artificial categorization of post/modernity, how self-expression, playfulness, and celebrity are enabled on a large and accessible scale for most people in the communities of both the "developed" and "undeveloped" worlds.

"So," I say, "what happened? Was that the end of Supla?"

"Nothing ever ends," says Trix. "I end things sometimes, but they never really end. If I'm lucky, things mostly just go away."

"You saw him again, then."

"He came by and then we went into town," she says. "The night before last. After a late dinner, we went to his place. It was fun. I bought a vibrator along the way, especially for the occasion."

"For size comparison?" I say. "One of the dildo kind?"

"You're bad," says Trix. "You really are."

"I am?"

"You just say things to get me to say things," she says. "You're a bad fucker."

And she laughs.

"But yes," she says, "I did do a little comparing. He won, hands down."

"He did?"

"Of course," says Trix. "What do you think?"

I write down, "vibrator...welding...postatomic rose/big green candle...space between skyscrapers..."

"Where does he live?"

"In town," says Trix, "on Avenue B between Twelfth and Thirteenth, a pretty dodgy part of town. He has a tiny place, a little apartment. With a cow's foot hanging outside his door."

"A what?"

"A cow's foot," says Trix. "A real cow's foot above the door and off to the left."

"To ward off evil spirits, I guess."

"I don't know," says Trix. "Probably. I didn't bother to ask its function. It was clean, though. It didn't smell. A beautiful hoof, with hair on it."

"A cow's foot," I say. "He probably brought it all the way from Brazil."

"He showed me lots of photos and newspaper clippings from Brazil," says Trix. "Pictures of him performing with Billy Idol, CD covers, fan club pictures, magazine layouts showing him performing at rock concerts, stuff like that. So, he must be pretty famous there."

"Yet he's here," I say, "on Avenue B, trying to look like a heavy metal rocker."

I write, "See Bhabha on mimicry..." I leaf through a book and jot down, "...to be effective, mimicry must continually produce its slippage, its excess, its difference."

"His place is pretty funky," says Trix. "The window is covered by this huge American flag and there are big leather whips draped over chairs and things, but the walls themselves are bare, nothing on them. I told him I liked the bare walls, and he said he did, too, but that they'd be even better when he put up some pictures. I asked him what kind of pictures and he said, 'Babes on Bikes.' Babes on Bikes, can you imagine? He said it like it was the most natural thing, like everybody has posters like that on their walls. For the first time I started thinking, let me out of here."

"Babes on Bikes?"

"I know," says Trix. "Believe me, I know. But, then, to be fair, under his pillow on his neatly made bed was a pair of perfectly folded black silk pajamas. So tidy it made me melt. And you know what he had on his boxer shorts?"

"No."

"Jumbo the elephant," says Trix. "Lots of little playful Jumbos. He has another pair with little green dinosaurs on them that glow in the dark. His mother gave them to him. His mother still gives him underpants. Dr. Ruth gives him underpants. How can you not like somebody like that? Somebody who wears baby dinosaurs under his studded leather?"

"Sounds like he might be a little confused," I say. "Like he skipped a couple of rungs on the cultural evolutionary ladder. That happens, when people move too quickly from there to here."

"He might make it, you know," says Trix. "His music is okay, and he's so fucking good-looking, tall, dark, and handsome."

" 'Touched by this swarthy tint spreading like an oil stain over the world,' " I say (Trinh 1991, p. 17).

"What?" says Trix.

"Something I'm reading," I say. "A quotation."

I page down on the computer, bringing up more of the rough draft.

That almost anyone has a chance to be on television, to gain a part in the movies, to participate in a talent show, to be spotlighted as an athlete, is quite specific to the present age. That this is so tells us a great deal about the present age as, to paraphrase Grossberg, a place of possible events; a voyage, a fantasy of future possibilities. One of the things Grossberg urges us to notice is how popular practices construct these places, how place constitutes what can happen. Within the third space celebrity, we can apply Grossberg's idea and note that the popular practices of celebrity are practices that do not just construct this place (1990s earth): they actually become this place. The place of possible events—the voyage, the fantasy, the untranslatable—thrives within celebrity. The practice and the geo-historical places of celebrity become world spaces, spaces that empower, spaces that restrict. The space of celebrity itself has become the signifier, the negative, the excess, the redemptive and more.

"It was fun," says Trix. "I enjoyed it a lot, but I've had enough of it."

"Of Supla?"

"Of Supla," says Trix.

"What happened?"

"Aaach," says Trix, "nothing, really."

"Come on," I say.

"Well," says Trix, "we were walking to his place and it was really late and really cold out. And we were walking fast. You know how fast I can walk, but he was walking faster, three or four paces ahead of me. He looked back and told me to hurry up. That's all. Just hurry up. And I said, 'Fuck you, I'm not a dog. Fuck you.' That's all. I just didn't like that, his tone of voice."

"When was this?"

"On the way to his apartment the other night."

"Just before the Babes on Bikes?"

"Yes," says Trix. "I know what you're thinking, but I decided I wouldn't let it spoil my evening. I mean, it wasn't really that big of a deal. I said fuck you to him a lot, just like I say it to you, to everybody. And we really had a great time that night. It was a lot of fun. But I kept thinking about it, his talking to me like I was a dog or something, a kaffir or something. I knew it'd never lead anywhere. He was also rude to the cab driver on the way into town. And he's a mean tipper. I mean, the little things kind of add up, when you think about them. So, I called him yesterday and I said I was sorry, but I didn't want any more of this, that I'd had a really good time and that's how I wanted to remember it."

"And?"

"And he said okay," says Trix. "He's really into his music. He'll handle it okay."

"And you?"

"Aach," says Trix, "you know me."

"So, you ended it."

"As best I could," says Trix. "With the memory still pleasant and sweet. Such a sweet little Brazilian boy."

She takes a deep drag on a cigarette, the inhalation loud and long. I hear a distant siren and the purr of a cat.

"So," she says, "what do you think I'm doing now?"

"Now? At 3:00 a.m.?" I say. "Besides talking to me?"

"Besides talking to you."

"I don't know."

"Guess," she says.

"Well," I say, "I'd say you are sitting on your love seat next to the red curtain and staring out your window at the subway stop, idly wondering if he might walk up the steps into the desolate green glare, wondering if you might discover wonder itself in his stare as he looks up toward the blood red light in your Long Island City window, wondering, perhaps, if he might serenade you in Portuguese, a soulful fado, maybe, a bittersweet lament."

I pull up the final paragraph of the rough draft:

The space of celebrity is not like the spaces that Spivak and others talk of; it is not opened, as Spivak asserts in her discussion of postcoloniality, by the colonizer, or by excess or negation. Further, the celebrity space is more than a liminal border space, more than a privileged moment. We want to work with the idea that celebrity spaces are what Grossberg would call the trope beyond that of Homi Bhabha, more closely allied to Rey Chow's ideas of spaces as those of exteriority, or possibility as event. For us, celebrity is a space that is "an experience that exhausts the resources of language," that begins to get outside the construction of difference;

a space that begins to play with and discard particular historical relations of power. The space of celebrity is culture itself, and this culture is, as Grossberg argues, a way of becoming.

I write down "-trix, suffix ... dict def: 1. female that does or is associated with a (specific) thing avia*trix*. 2. geometric line, point, surface genera*trix* ... "

"Is that about right?" I say.

"Fuck you," says Trix. And then she laughs and says, "I know you love it when I say that."

"I do," I say. "Among other things, I guess it helps me feel a part of it all."

"And you still long for that?"

"Still and always," I say. "Just like you. Except you still do something about it, every once in a while. Which is more than I can say for me."

"Well, fuck."

"Fuck," I say, "is right."

Note

1. See Nate Kohn and Synthia S. Slowikowski (1994), "Look at Us Now: Celebrity and the Third Space," unpublished paper presented at the Society for the Study of Symbolic Interaction Annual Meetings session on Postmodernism and Cultural Studies II, Los Angeles.

A man looking out of an open window never sees as much as the same man looking directly at a closed window. There is no object more deeply mysterious, no object more pregnant with suggestion, more insidiously sinister, in short more truly dazzling than a window lit up from within by even a single candle. What we can see out in the sunlight is always less interesting than what we can perceive taking place behind a pane of window-glass. In that pit, in that blackness or brightness, life is being lived, life is suffering, life is dreaming. . . .

—Charles Baudelaire, *The Flowers of Evil*

Picking out images from my soul's eye, fishing for the right words to recreate the images. Words are blades of grass pushing past the obstacles, sprouting on the page; the spirit of the words moving in the body is as concrete as flesh and as palpable; the hunger to create is as substantial as finger and hand. I look at my fingers, see plumes growing there.

—Gloria Anzaldúa, *Borderlands/La Frontera*

It becomes possible to understand the basis of the distrust of totalizing systems of knowledge which depend upon theory and concepts, so characteristic of Foucault or Lyotard, both of whom have been predominantly concerned with the attempt to isolate and foreground singularity as opposed to universality. This quest for the singular, the contingent event which by definition refuses all conceptualization, can clearly be related to the project of constructing a form of knowledge that respects the other without absorbing it into the same.

—Robert Young, *White Mythologies: Writing History and the West*

9

Compounding Fracture

"I means you."

"Don't talk like an illiterate person."

"That's not what I mean. I mean I means you, like I stands for you, I am you, but more, much more. It's an endearment with deep structural, some might say semiotic significance."

"Oh, okay."

"A sort of Derridean deconstruction of endearments, even."

"I'm supposed to reply to that? You want me to reply to that?"

"You could say, 'Thank you.'"

"Thank you."

"You could say 'I means you, too.'"

"I could. But I won't. Just because you say something doesn't mean I have to say something too."

"Maybe you're right."

"Certain things are sometimes best left unsaid. Unthought, even."

"I said you were right."

"Maybe. You said maybe I was right."

"I always say maybe."

"Yes, you do. You're a real maybe kind of guy."

"When I was in the airport in Chicago that guru woman, the one with the bleached hair, the one who used to be a fat housewife and now does those absolutely loud and exhausting exercise infomercials on TV—you know the one I mean . . ."

"I don't remember her name but I know the one you mean. From way back when. Not the buns of steel people, the other one."

"Right, the same vintage. That one, the one with the philosophy, the one you'd think would be dead by now, or at least forgotten."

"Apparently not yet. At least not by you."

"I'm trying to forget, believe me."

"You say you forget everything—"

"Only sometimes. But listen: I'm rushing between G and K concourse and I hear this loud Jersey voice saying, 'Shit, something's got to be open, for Christ's sake,' the sound cutting through the din, piercing it, like, I don't know, an ice cutter through ice. I turn around and there she is, a baggy shirt hanging off one bare shoulder, breasts bouncing, flunkies trailing, mouth going a mile a minute chewing gum. Nostrils flared, she rushes past me, like I wasn't even there, expensive bags hanging off her, more expensive bags hanging off the two girls gliding in her wake, chins out, a wedge of female flesh in search of some necessary and urgent item in the wee hours of an O'Hare morning."

"You paint a lovely picture."

"I try. Clifford Geertz. Thick description. You know, the emphasis on 'thick.'"

"Emphasizing your thickness again. Love it when you do that."

"Irony? Are you being ironical? Saying one thing when you mean the opposite? Because if you are . . . "

"See what I mean: thick."

"Can I just finish my narrative? Please? Distraction, you know, is well-theorized hegemonic sleight of hand."

"All I said was 'You paint a lovely picture.' You said everything else. You distract you, not me. Or should I say, not I?"

"Now that's a distraction."

"Got me. You got me again. Caught me in a distraction."

"Okay. Thank you. Now just let me finish, okay?"

"Okay, okay."

So, then she says, 'Shit, shit, shit,' on seeing that another shop is not open. She stops suddenly, her white hair bristly, her nostrils expanding in centimeters as if about to give birth. 'This fucking country,' she says, putting the accent on the 'fucking.' Her shoulder is very white, alabaster, ivory, smooth, her collar-bone pronounced and parallel to the floor, her waist home to bands of gold and works of oriental art, her heart pounding in her chest, her nipples pointed up toward the flags hanging from the ceiling, her pupils dilating before my eyes. In a very loud voice, she again says, 'Shit, shit, shit.' Then she rushes back past me, leaving the two girls behind, momentarily detaching her retinue—"

"Jesus, you didn't go all this way for that pun, that old pun, Jesus."

"What do you take me for? What do you think? Of course—"

"Never mind."

"You want to hear the rest of it? Because if you don't—"

"You got me on pins and needles."

"Don't you wish."

"Asshole."

"I know."

"Needles, I said, and pins."

"So, she rushes back past me—"

"Powter, that's her name. Susan Powter. And she's from Australia or someplace, not New Jersey."

"Did I say Jersey?"

"You said Jersey accent."

"Ah."

"Don't ah me. Don't give me those absurd theoretical distinctions. Don't do that."

"Did I do that?"

"You do it all the time these days. You were going to do it again."

"Well, I might have been thinking about it. Traveling cultures, transplanted accents, that sort of thing. A little James Clifford, maybe."

"Don't. Just finish your story. Just finish it."

"Well, Susan Powter—that's her name, Australian with Hoboken accent—well, her two girls exchange a look, take synchronous deep breaths and follow her. As they pass me, one says to the other, 'So she leaves a trail of blood from here to Tampa, who cares, she's a star, for Christ's sake.' And the other one says, 'They should be down on their hands and knees licking it up.'"

"What? They said that?"

"They did. To each other. 'Down on their hands and knees . . .' I overheard. I remembered. I am telling you."

"Wow."

"That's what I thought. Wow. Spelled backwards."

"You realize I'll never be able to watch her again without it coming to mind, without that disgusting image plaguing me."

"I've implanted a new schemata in your mind. Feel yourself lucky, privileged, empowered."

"You can be so kind. When you try."

"It *is* irony. You are being ironical with me, trying to mimic me, trying to rob me of my ironical domain. I recognize irony when I see it. When you hurl it in my face. I do. Baudrillard says that the subtle layer of irony is what protects us from the radiation of stupidity. And he says it's fast disappearing. I'm glad to see it's still alive and well with you."

"And I'm glad you're glad."

"Are you really?"

"Glad you think me completely stupid."

"Did I say that? Did I? Did I ever?"

"A friend of mine works in a hospital, the maternity ward, where people have babies."

"I know what the maternity ward is."

"I know you know. I was just reaffirming it for myself. I need to do that sometimes. Words get shorn of meaning, you know, shorn. Angela McRobbie's word: shorn. Sometimes I have to sew them back on."

"You never sewed anything in your life. Maybe that McRobbie woman has, but not you. Not your kind of needling."

"A pun. You said a pun. And I thought I was the only one with a penchant for punning."

"Penchant?"

"Penchant. Proclivity. Propensity. Appetite. Bent."

"Bent?"

"Never mind. How can your mimicry turn everything so ... so parenthetical?"

"Distraction, I was recently told, is—"

"Stop it."

"If you insist. Anyhow ... "

"Anyhow, there is this black woman with a new baby girl, jet black dressed in pink. My friend says something like, 'Cute baby,' and the woman says, 'Ain't she, though,' and my friend looks at the name tag on the baby and it reads, 'Female Washington,' and my friend says to the mother, 'What's her name?' and the mother says, 'That be it,' and my friend says, 'Did you name her?' and the woman says, 'They done named her,' and my friend says, 'You like it?' and the woman says, 'Ain't bad, kinda pretty,' and then she looks at the baby with evident love and pride and says, 'Female Washington.' Only she pronounces Female with three syllables, like it rhymes with tamale, as in hot tamale. Fe-mal-e. Imagine that."

"I'm trying not to."

"Says something about something, about the power of naming, hegemony at work in everyday life ... "

"If you say so."

"I could have told it as a joke, I didn't have to tell it the way I did, I could have turned it into a goddam Rasmus and Remus joke for Christ's sake."

"You're so considerate of the feelings of others."

"Irony should be subtle, you know. Description is thick, irony is subtle."

"It is a joke, though. I've heard it before, as a joke, a trite, bad, racist joke. I've heard variations on it, other puns. It's beyond me that you believed it was true. Shows me a whole new side to you—"

"Why the hell didn't you stop me? Why?"

"Do I ever stop you? Do I ever?"

"So there I was, standing with Ally McBeal and Michelle Pfeiffer, right next to the bar in the Grand Ballroom. At the Waldorf."

"Ally McBeal's a character. You were standing with the actress—"

"Real names don't matter in television. In television, actors become their characters. Disappear into their characters, for good and without desperation. Frasier is Frasier, for God's sake, not some actor. And Ally's Ally—"

"Something Flockhart—"

"I was standing with Ally, not *somebody* called *something*. Jerry Seinfeld understood. That's why he named his character Jerry Seinfeld. In movies, on the other hand, actors never become their characters. The crisis of representation is alive and well in the movies. Not TV. TV's the postmodern condition. Fluid, fractured, seducing, exposed, all-consuming, sublime."

"It probably says Ally McBeal on her driver's license. On her passport."

"It probably does. And if it doesn't, it should."

"Jesus Christ."

"And the funny thing was they both looked so much alike, Ally and Michelle. Smooth white skin, like porcelain, but soft silky porcelain, unlike any porcelain in the mundane world, the same warm look on both of them, absolutely perfect complexion, bone structure, lips, teeth brilliant white, blonde hair razor cut, eyes sparkling, and that star aura radiating, absolutely dazzling, that Benjaminian aura, fuzzy, warm, seductive, turning the whole room pink, Jayne Mansfield pink."

"Rose colored, more likely—"

"Michelle wore heavy black plastic–rimmed glasses. That was the only difference. I wanted to reach up and take them off—"

"I bet that's not all you wanted."

"I was swooning, I admit, so filled with gawk. They were beautifully perfect mirrors of each other, so touchable, welcoming, so three-dimensional, their subtle perfumes filling the air, tickling my nostrils. So delicate, Ally and Michelle, so regal, so confident, so at ease in the world."

"Even with you right there, sweating."

"Even with."

"Even with them looking right through you."

"I smiled. They smiled back. I was there in the room with them, at the Waldorf. I was one of them; I was somebody too. There, in that moment."

"That's pathetic. Absolutely pathetic."

"Maybe so, but it wasn't in that moment. It was a moment unlike any other. Satisfaction was complete."

"Really?"

"Really."

"I don't know why I listen to you anymore."

"You had to be there. If you had been, you'd understand."

"You've crossed over. You really have. You're one of them now."

"There is no us and them, no binary, not anymore, not in the television age, not in a postmodern world. There's only us and us."

"Right. Only us. Thank God for 'only us.'"

"You messing with me, aren't you? Don't do this to me. Don't."

"I'm not doing anything."

"You're saying and saying's doing."

"Saying's saying."

"Saying's doing. The utterance. The speech act. Performativity. Austin and Bakhtin. Don't you know anything?"

"Clearly not as much as you."

"Clearly."

"You know what I want on my tombstone? Engraved on it?"

"'Fuck 'em if they can't take a joke?'"

"Well, no. I want 'He used big words like he knew what they meant.'"

"You do. Really?"

"I do."

"What about, 'What's love got to do with it, do with it, do with it?'"

"That's a possibility, maybe. But it's not original. I didn't think of it. It should be something I thought of, something from me, like what I just said, like 'He used big words like he knew what they meant.' Now that's really me. I like that. Captures my ironical postmodern turn."

"Really."

"Really. Really me."

"I guess it would probably be best if I didn't make suggestions."

"It probably would, yes. Not in matters like this."

"I won't, then."

"Then don't."

"Okay."

"All right."

"How about, 'Like his fifteen minutes of fame, his life was over before it began.'"

"Very funny."

"It gave me a brief chuckle."

"I thought you weren't going to help."

"I didn't. I made a joke. Forget it."

"How can I forget it? It was so vicious."

"Believe me, you can forget it. You forget most things."

"Paul Virilio says the more there is to know, the less you know, the more you forget. The more you have to forget."

"And Paul should know, I'm sure."

"I'm contemplating immortality here."

"I'm sorry. I didn't realize. A serious moment, then. I'll be appropriately solemn."

"Thank you."

"The least I can do."

"Okay. So, now, it'll either be 'He used big words like he knew what they meant,' or, how about this, 'Born blind, he will be remembered for a mendacious and deceptive clear-sightedness.'"

"Mendacious... If I were to say you were a mendacious asshole, would that be a correct use of the word?"

"Mendacious is not a big word. Everybody uses it. Even Clinton uses it. Even people talking about Clinton use it. And no, that would not be a correct use of the word. I could be an asshole, but I—me, personally—cannot be a mendacious asshole. Now you, given your particular standpoint—your peculiar standpoint— you might want to read me that way—and you can certainly do that—but that is not the privileged reading. No one would say that is the privileged reading."

"I'm not talking to you any more."

"You're not?"

"No."

"Why? Why not? What did I say? What?"

To face reality squarely and sensitively, without positive or negative escapism, is to see "the small in the large and the large in the small; the real in the illusory and the illusory in the real" (Shen-Fu).

—Trinh Minh-ha, *When the Moon Waxes Red*

Lately returned from the valley of the shadow of death, he is rapturously breathing in all the odours and essences of life; as he has been on the brink of total oblivion, he remembers, and fervently desires to re-member, everything. Finally he hurls himself headlong into the midst of the throng, in pursuit of an unknown, half-glimpsed countenance that has, on an instant, be-witched him. Curiosity has become a fatal, irresistible passion!

—Charles Baudelaire, *The Painter of Modern Life*

10

Elementary Africa

Reading the newspaper and watching *Rugrats* with my daughter, an episode called "The Big House," where Tommy, a mere toddler, is locked up with some rough-looking convicts, all in diapers, some with suspenders, others with three-day growths. An amusing parody of the Wallace Beery film, I am thinking, something my four-year-old must be appreciating for its gently nostalgic aura, I am thinking, when the phone rings...

"Hey, how you doin'?" It's Harry. "Long fuckin' time, huh?"

"Harry," I say.

Harry never has to announce himself, say his name, his raspy voice saving him the trouble, giving him an enunciatory trademark known on at least three continents.

"Sooooooooooo," says Harry, "how's things?"

On the TV, Tommy is lying on his cot, next to a couple of other toddler convicts, musing as convicts do just before lights-out, Tommy saying that he's got a woman waitin' for him on the outside, too...his mom!

"Remember Cagney in *White Heat*?" I say.

"I don't," says Harry, "but I'm sure my mommy does."

"Jesus, Harry."

"How long's it been?" says Harry. "Can't remember the last time I called, at least a year, huh. That's right, the *Arkansas Spring* revival thing. That fell flat on its ass, big time. As I remember, you weren't needed in New York after all."

119

"Where are you now, Harry?" I say. "Whose phone are you on?"

A raspy laugh and a cough.

"New York," says Harry. "A doctor friend of mine's place on the Upper West Side. Just got back from six months in Kenya, in what I like to call deep isolation, getting some writing done, you know..."

In the newspaper I am reading Mike's restaurant review of a place called Campus View, a former Mr. Steak. Mike's still in his second year of law school, making a little extra money writing reviews of local eateries.

Mike: "I experienced a curious sense of *deja vu*. Campus View has the same sofa-sized art hanging on its walls, comfortable booths and a geriatric ward feel that provide a peculiar sense of security..."

"Good to hear your voice, Harry," I hear myself saying. "Good to know you're still out there hustling, that maybe there still are a few constants in the world after all."

"Hey, what the fuck," says Harry. "You about done with that school shit? Got that PhD tucked away in your hip pocket yet?"

"Just finished my prelims—"

"That like orals?"

"Written and oral," I say. "I'm working on my dissertation."

"Yeah," says Harry, "I figured you should be about done. What's the dissertation on?"

"The pursuit of celebrity," I say. "You know, how some people can't get away from wanting to be in the movies and on TV, like it's an addiction or something, an obsession..."

"I wouldn't have thought that five-six years ago," says Harry, "but, shit, I get back from Africa, the middle of fucking nowhere, and the first thing I want to know is what's going on in the business. The election, Haiti, health care, I could give a fuck. How Woody got on with Oliver Stone, now that was my very first phone call."

"I know," I say. "That's what I'm writing about."

"And they let you get away with that shit?" says Harry, with the gurgle of liquid being poured in the background. "You going to some kind of correspondence school or something?"

Tommy is pumping iron with what looks like barbells made out of Legos and bent erector set parts. Other toddler prisoners walk around looking bored and trying to whistle, while a guard taunts Tommy with no pain no gain.

"You know what I've been thinking a lot about lately, Harry," I say. "I've been remembering my first trip to Europe, right out of high school, back in the early sixties. I went to Vienna because that's where my father was from and what hit me first off was how the streets were filled with blind people and cripples, old people without arms and legs, with limbs missing. They were war victims, I finally figured out, World War Two victims, still hobbling around, barely mobile testaments to the horror of war almost twenty years after the fact. I bet they weren't thinking about how Orson Welles got along with Carol Reed when they were making *The Third Man*."

"Maybe not," says Harry. "But, hell, if they'd had Oprah back then, I bet you dollars to donuts they'd be busting their balls to get on her show, tell the intimate story about how that Allied bomb gimped 'em."

"We just don't see stuff like that anymore on the streets," I say. "We forget. It's on TV, but it's not the same. We forget."

"Shit, man," says Harry. "You want to see that stuff? Try Nairobi or Mogadishu or Kampala. Go to Rwanda. Hell, the Germans are now bringing in groups of tourists to look at the piles of dead bodies, for Christ's sake. Fuck, man, you have been stuck in the corn fields too long."

"Maybe," I say. "Maybe..."

Tommy and his fellow inmates are complaining about the food now, banging their plastic spoons on the table. A sadistic-looking warden peers malevolently at them from behind a barred window.

"*Natural Born Killers*," says Harry. "What did you think?"

"Not a whole lot."

"Biggest piece of horseshit," says Harry. "Woody looked okay, but every time he opened his mouth I about shit in my pants. I mean, you call that acting?"

"Posing as acting," I say. "Posing in motion as acting. Speed as acting. Speed is everything. Not stopping, ever."

"And that speech at the end," says Harry. "Who's Stone think he's kidding?"

"A little heavy-handed," I say. "In case you missed the point, here it is again, for the forty-first time."

"Fuckin' right," says Harry. "Makes my blood boil, what's left of it."

Mike, in the newspaper, still writing about the Campus View eatery, commenting on its ambiance, how it reminds him of being in a time warp circa 1973.

"So," I say, "what's happening? What's new with you, then, Harry?"

"Funny you should ask," says Harry.

I can hear him taking a sip of something, lubricating the throat and the mind at the same time.

"I was in Kenya," says Harry, "staying with a friend of mine up around Garissa near the Sudanese border, really in the middle of fucking nowhere, beautiful country, about as far from ugly as you can get. I was doing some writing, working on a book, really getting some writing done, fucking nice stuff—"

"A novel?"

"Well, no, not really," says Harry. "I'm writing about how I went about getting some of the stories I got, what happened to me when I was doing the reporting. You know, when I was working for *Life* magazine and *Harper's*, those guys. I'll tell you, chasing the stories was a hell of a lot more interesting than the stories themselves. How I got the Breytenbach interview, all that South African intrigue, my visits to Leavenworth to talk to that murderer about *Arkansas Spring*, getting Ian Smith to spill his guts, stuff like that."

"Sort of like a memoir," I say.

"I guess," says Harry. "Except I got something like three hundred pages already and I'm only up to my fifteenth birthday. Going to be a fucking long book."

"All good stuff, no doubt," I say.

"Hey," says Harry, "I edit. I fucking edit, for Christ's sake."

Tommy is now conspiring with his fellow diapered inmates to break out of the big house. They can't take it anymore—the intimidation, the food, the constant surveillance, the indiscriminate time-outs. It's more than they can stand.

"You worry every word to death," I say. "You always have. And once you kill it, it stays there dead on the page forever."

"Taking a few literary criticism courses, are we," says Harry. "The word *reify* wouldn't be itching to cross your tongue about now, would it? Or, better, *reifi-fucking-cation.*"

Harry laughs.

"Jesus, Harry."

"You already said that once," says Harry.

"And I'll probably say it forty-one more times before we're done," I say.

"Well, hell," says Harry. "Why don't you just let me finish the story about how your name came up in the middle of the African wilderness, okay?"

"My name?"

"Your name," says Harry. "Honest to fucking god."

"Well . . . " I say.

"We were at my friend's house on the edge of the escarpment, all of Africa in its virgin splendor spilling outward from the bougainvilleaed veranda as far as the eye can see, heaving hills tumbling down toward Mombasa and the Indian Ocean, herds of giraffe—"

"Stop it, Harry."

"A little color is all," says Harry as he chokes on a swallow of something, "setting the mood."

"Who's your friend?"

"Barry?" says Harry. "About my age. A limey. He's lived in Kenya for twenty years or more. Used to be a publisher in London, had a small press somewhere in Soho. Made his first money publishing the beat poets, I think—"

"Ferlinghetti?"

"Him," says Harry, "and Ginsberg. Maybe some Kerouac and some Paul Bowles, I can't remember. Anyhow, Jonathan Cape bought him out in the early seventies, just before the oil embargo thing, the big crash, and he took the money and moved out there. Has two houses, another one just outside Nairobi. Hell of a great guy."

"Anybody who lets you stay with him for six months is a hell of a great guy. Particularly anybody with a well-stocked bar and fridge."

"Ain't that the fucking truth," says Harry.

"You're an open book, Harry," I say. "One we've all read before."

"But, hey," says Harry, "I keep 'em laughing. I got a million tales to tell and all that shit. I'm cheap at the fucking price. I'm better than a dog, a pipe, a fire, and a dog-eared Agatha Christie, for Christ's sake."

"You're a great guy, Harry."

"Well," says Harry, "you know. I'm still out there, still kicking in doors and asking questions."

"Sure," I say. "Sure you are, Harry."

Tommy has a girl toddler fashioning a key to the prison door out of Play-Doh while he's whispering some kind of instructions to another toddler, this one with bright orange hair. The Play-Doh is golden in color and takes on the shape of the Statue of Liberty before the girl squeezes it into a ball and starts to give it the form of a key.

"Anyhow," says Harry, the click of a cigarette lighter punctuating a short pause, "we're at a friend of Barry's house near Nairobi not far from Peter Beard's permanent safari camp watching some videos. Most of them you couldn't make head nor tail of, like looking at the screen through the bottom of a fucking pie plate or something. But, then, Barry's friend puts on one and it's clear as day and there, big as life on the screen, is your fucking name. 'Produced by Nate Kohn' big as fucking life on the thirty-one-inch Sony in the middle of the African bush. *Zulu Dawn*, first time I actually saw the thing. Hell of an impressive movie. Knocked those guys' fucking snake boots off. Quite a moment, I tell you, when I said that guy's a friend of mine, we almost made a movie together."

"I have a sinking feeling this is leading somewhere, Harry," I say.

"Fucking great movie, man," says Harry. "If you'd said something about how good it is I might have watched it years ago. I mean, it's a goddam epic, cast of thousands, right up there with *Lawrence-of-fucking-Arabia*. You even got Peter O'Toole in there, for Christ's sake."

"Harry—"

"So, anyhow, we got talking again about making movies in Kenya, me and Barry and his friend. They're in the advertising business over there, him and Barry, among other things, and every time a production company comes through from Europe or the States they buy some equipment off them if they can—cameras, lights, costumes, stuff like that. A lot of guys would rather sell their stuff than lug it back stateside, particularly after it's been dropped off the back of a damn elephant or something. So, over the years, they've built up quite a good little studio, fully equipped and all."

"Remember what I told you last time, Harry?" I say. "About getting back in the business? About the sour taste in my mouth? About that *Arkansas Spring* fiasco, the one you visited upon me?"

"Hell," says Harry, "things change. Time changes things. Water under the fucking bridge and all. Shit, you sound like a new person, all that fucking tension's out of your voice. School's almost out, you gotta be chomping at the bit. What you going to do? Teach fucking Foucault for the rest of your life? Hell, man, listen to the deal for fuck's sake, give it a chance, it ain't so bad."

Mike finishes his piece about the Campus View hoping it will improve and find an identity of its own. He thinks there is always room for a restaurant that understands how to do simple things well.

"I know a guy here," I say, "who is in law school, you know, studying to be a lawyer. Name's Mike. What he really wants to be is a writer, but he knows he can't make a living at that. He also wouldn't mind being a cook, but that's not easy to support a family, either, so now he's in law school and hating every minute of it. What he really likes is his part-time job writing reviews of restaurants for the local newspaper. He likes it so much that he spends more time on it than he should and his studies are suffering. For sixty dollars a week and the satisfaction of seeing his words in print."

"Am I supposed to find something in that for me," says Harry, "'cause if I am, it just flew by me like so much horseshit out of Trigger's ass."

"Never mind," I say. "I wasn't talking to you, really, I was talking to myself, maybe trying out a new space for myself, just seeing if I split the difference, occupy a space in between, maybe—"

"Hey, man," says Harry between gulps, "I haven't the foggiest idea what you're talking about, but I'm talking about fucking Africa. Africa is space. All the space you'll ever need. A fucking spatial paradise, one of the last few left on this shithole we call earth."

"Yeah, Harry," I say. "I know. I've been there."

"Just stop wanking, man," says Harry. "For Christ's sake, listen to me. These guys say they can raise the cash needed as well, like maybe two million dollars U.S. equivalent, in addition to the equipment they already own. And they can—these guys are wired in, believe me, fucking wired in."

On the TV, the orange-haired toddler suddenly fakes a trip and falls to the ground where he starts crying in an exaggerated frenzy. All three prison guards rush to him and stand around him, gawking. His mouth is open wide, cavernously large, larger than his head. The camera zooms inside, his vibrating little tongue filling the screen as he screams and cries uncontrollably.

"So they want me to write the scripts and you to produce the fucking films, 'cause they know fuck-all about producing and they know I drink like a fish and am about as organized as Bill fucking Clinton and they really loved your movie. Believe me, these guys aren't bullshitters. Hell, they don't have to be, they already made theirs, they're just looking to have a little fun, maybe help some guys they know move a little money."

With the prison guards distracted, Tommy directs the rest of the inmates as they build a mountainous tower out of blocks, a staircase toward the keyhole in the prison door. A line of toddlers forms and the blocks get passed in record speed.

"Where," I hear myself saying, "is the cash coming from, then."

"Asians, mainly," says Harry. "They got all the cash in Kenya, and they're desperate to get it out of the country. Both the Africans and the British treat 'em like dirt. Always have, always will. Look at what Amin did to them. The fucking Jews of Africa, the poor bastards. Hell, there's no better way to move money than with a movie. And they know that, smart little buggers, those fucking Indians."

"Yeah," I say, "I know all about it, too, Harry. Bundles of humid cash, dank banknotes held together with rusty paper clips and wrapped in pastel tissue paper held together with sticky tape. Somebody's life savings out of a galvanized box buried under a banyan tree. I did that in South Africa, with some Pakistanis. Really sad."

"Fucking sad," says Harry. "But, hey, we're here to fucking help."

"A strange compulsion to help the needy whose needs we participated in creating," I say.

"What?" says Harry.

"Nothing," I say.

"Don't go soppy on me here, man," says Harry, a violent sloshing sound in the background. "Don't go theoretical, don't go sounding like they've brainwashed you, for Christ's sake."

"Just paraphrasing Trinh Minh-ha," I say. "It seemed to apply. There's this other writer who also applies, named Homi Bhabha. He says that the critic must attempt to realize fully and take responsibility for the unspoken, unrepresented pasts that haunt the historical present. We're critics, Harry. We have responsibilities."

"Homi who?" says Harry.

"Homi Bhabha," I say. "A postcolonial writer."

"Any relation to Ali?" says Harry. "And his forty thieves?"

The tower of blocks completed, a pudgy toddler with a spotty three-day growth and a beer belly hanging over his diaper top starts to climb, his full diaper coming from behind frame, up and over the camera, in a dramatically constructed assent. He reaches the top and calls for the key. Tommy hurls it up to him, and he fumbles the catch, almost dropping it, before securing it in his grasp at the last possible moment.

"What's the story, Harry?" I say. "Have you written it yet?"

"Fuck, no," says Harry, his words starting to slur slightly. "I told them I can't write it until they pay me Writer's Guild minimum. I mean, you know, I'd write the thing on spec if I could, but William Morris would never let me. I told them that, and they said no problem, no fucking problem, as long as most of the elements are in place."

"Like me," I say.

"You're an element," says Harry. "Like hydrogen or lead or fucking uranium. One of the lucky diners at the elementary table."

The fat toddler reaches up to fit the key in the keyhole, but it's just out of his reach, slightly too high. He cries that he can't reach it. Tommy, glancing over to see the warders still occupied with the distracting redhead, tells the fat toddler that maybe he can reach if he stands on his shoulders. And Tommy begins to climb the mountain, his bulging diaper now advancing dramatically through the frame.

"The story, Harry."

"Well," says Harry, "up in the north of Kenya, there are these bandits that raid down from the Sudan, real ugly mothers who ride camels and terrorize the locals. Quite a problem over there. Well, a Ted Turner–type businessman is over on holiday or something and he happens to witness a raid on a group of Masai. He watches dumbfounded as four Masai warriors chase down the bandits on foot, running like the wind like only they can do, overtaking the fleeing camels, and capturing the bastards. The speed mesmerizes him. So, he gets this idea of taking them to the states and entering them in the Drake Relay Race—"

"Drake College?" I say. "In Des Moines, Iowa?"

"The very same. World-fucking-famous race."

"Harry—"

"But they never make it to Des Moines. They get stuck in New York working for a messenger service and all kinds of really funny things happen."

Tommy is now at the top of the mountain, and he scampers up and onto the shoulders of the fat toddler. He takes the key and arches up toward the keyhole. The key, full in frame, inches toward the hole as Tommy almost loses his balance. Finally, insertion is achieved, the door swings open wide. And there stands Tommy's mother, a big smile on her face, her arms reaching out to him. And suddenly, the ominous penitentiary dissolves into an innocuous daycare center, complete with friendly, helpful daycare workers.

"Jesus Christ, Harry," I say.

"Just kidding," says Harry.

"You fucking better be," I say.

"Hey," says Harry. "I make it up as I go along. What the hell."

"So," I hear myself saying, "do we all. But this time I'm going to make it up right. And I'm going to make sure you make it up right, too."

"Whatever, man," says Harry. "Simmer down. The story'll be fine. You don't have to worry. Hell, I got a million of them."

"I'm going to worry it to death, Harry," I say. "Me and Homi Bhabha and the forty thieves."

"Jesus, man," says Harry.

"That's the deal," I say.

"Like I said," says Harry, "whatever."

"Whatever," I say.

"Okay," says Harry. "You got a fucking deal. You can worry it to death. Fill your fucking space with worry if you want. You got a fucking deal, man. We got a deal."

"Nice," I say, "when the negotiation's over before you know it's even begun, huh, Harry?"

"Fucking wonderful," says Harry.

"Be in touch, okay, Harry?"

"Yeah," says Harry. "You fucking bet."

And, with a deftness and a lightness I thought long gone, I return the receiver to its cradle.

"Daddy?"

It's my daughter's voice. I look at her.

"Daddy," she says, "Tommy's not in jail anymore."

"I know," I say.

And then I start to tell her about Africa . . .

PART III

DREAD

To listen, to see like a stranger in one's own land; to fare like a foreigner across one's own language; or, to maintain an intense rapport with the means and materiality of media languages is also to learn to let go of the (masterly) "hold" as one unbuilds and builds. It is, to borrow a metaphor by Toni Morrison "what the nerves and the skin remember as well as how it appears. And a rush of imagination is our 'flooding.' " What she wishes to leave the reader/view with, finally, is not so much a strong message, nor a singular story, but as Tchicaya U Tam'si puts it, "the fire and the song."

—Trinh Minh-ha, *When the Moon Waxes Red*

I am cold. I am singing voicelessly.... I am writing to go beyond myself; but what anguish if I succeed. Far away from myself. I can only bear this anguish if you will please take me in your arms.

—Helene Cixous, *The Helene Cixous Reader*

11

Messing

FADE IN:

BLACK SCREEN. SILENCE. Then

              YOUR VOICE (VOICE-OVER)
    Two questions constantly occur to me:
    What would this look like filmed? What
    would the soundtrack be?[1]

A BEAT OF BLACK, then

                                    CUT TO:

INT. BEDROOM   EARLY MORNING

CLOSE ON
Your sleeping face, in bed. Your head on a rumpled
pillow, eyes tightly shut, not a relaxed face. No
movement. A still picture except for muted colored
lights that flicker slowly across your face in the
early predawn light, barely perceptible emittances
from a silent television set somewhere in the
room.

Suddenly, your eyes open. Wide, but blurry, laced
with the sticky greenish cobwebs of sleep,
remnants of tears, viruses, infection. A frozen
expectant terror.

A second after your eyes open, the sudden blaring
SOUND of a clock radio clicking on, followed by
Willie Nelson's voice, instantly loud, singing:

>   WILLIE ON RADIO (V.O.)
>   Got to accentuate the positive,
>   eliminate the negative...

CLOSER ON
Your single blinking eye, bloodshot and unrested,
red-veined and pussy yellow, still trapped behind
a lattice of sticky, hardening green sleep. With
difficulty, the eye closes.

>   CUT TO:

BLACK SCREEN. Sudden silence. Then a single
crystal clear lidless eye, a hyperreal
computer-generated high-resolution model perhaps,
all surfaces thinly coated in a clear, shining,
reflective liquid, quickly FADES IN, sharp and
inquiring, suspended in the blackness, not unlike
the eye from Kubrick's *2001: A Space Odyssey*.

Throughout these BLACK SCREEN sequences that
punctuate the film, the CAMERA roves fluidly in
and around this hyperreal eye, exploring its many
surfaces from every possible angle. And always
reflected in mirror image or inverted or both on
these many eye surfaces are seas of texts,
including those being read by the VOICE, pages of
upside-down or backward words swimming across
lubricated iris, cornea, retina, nerve endings,
blood vessels, an efficient unrelenting scanning
that the CAMERA moves across, around, and through
with an irrepressible fluidity, an absolute
impunity.

The VOICE reading these words is in fact many
single voices that seamlessly morph into each
other every few seconds with the continuity of
meaning never disturbed. A woman's voice becomes a
boy's voice becomes a Southern voice becomes an

announcer's voice becomes a German-accented voice, and so on. This unending succession of seemingly arbitrary voices comes across as one voice reading in all these BLACK SCREEN sequences.

> VOICE (V.O.)
> It was the tiredness of time lived, with its days and days. It was the tiredness of gravity.... He was in a terrible state—that of consciousness. Some while ago in his life he had lost the knack of choosing what to think about.[2]

CUT TO:

INT. BEDROOM   EARLY MORNING   CONTINUING

CLOSE ON
Your blurry bloodshot eye, wide open, crusted sleep in the corner.

> WILLIE ON RADIO (V.O., CONTINUING)
> Got to spread joy up to the maximum....

P.O.V. of your bloodshot eye:
A partial image, blocked by a blurred round of nose, a fuzzy line twisting across the screen behind which is an oddly disproportional expanse of bed, a closely seen terrain devoid of known markers. It could be any place, any time, a land either foreign or familiar, depending on the vagaries of mood, memory, pain—a damp, wrinkled sheet up close (sweat maybe, or rain, or tears), then large mountains of quilt, vast valleys, peaks and twists and knots, with a gray duvet rising like snow mass in the far background. Still the flicker of television light as the only movement, an unnatural light, shallow yellows and greens and pinks evaporating over the frozen, fuzzy, fluffy landscape.

> WILLIE ON RADIO (V.O., CONTINUING)
> Yes, we've got to accentuate—

Your eye, open, motionless and bloodshot, dark red
rivers in a desert of yellow, staring through the
cobwebs of green. A tear in the corner, forming,
not yet heavy enough to drop.

CUT TO:

BLACK SCREEN. Sudden silence. Then the pristine
eye and morphing VOICE, CAMERA exploring as
before.

VOICE (V.O.)

> If a new song grabs my heart, I'll
> typically play it over and over and over
> again until it's completely robbed of
> all significance, beauty and power.[3]

CUT TO:

INT. KITCHEN   MORNING

CLOSE ON
Television blaring on top of the refrigerator.
Images of dead bodies being hauled out of a mass
grave.

REPORTER (V.O.)

> ...recently discovered just outside
> Tuzla. At least two hundred fifty
> bodies, some children...

You (glasses, bleary-eyed, middle-aged) open the
freezer door, dig for the yellow Eggo box. A
cordless phone is cradled between your shoulder
and ear. You glance up at the television.

YOU
(into phone)

> Mr. In Between, Harry. That's what
> Jonathan is, and we've got to stop
> messing with him. He's like those guys
> in Kenya, all sizzle and no steak, last

month's major waste of everybody's time.
Just go straight to the money man, latch
on to the affirmative....

Two Eggos in hand, you move toward the toaster.

              REPORTER (V.O.)
...directly at the feet of the Bosnian
Serbs...
                YOU
             (into phone)
Willie Nelson, on the radio, you know,
with that omnipresent hint of
melancholy, weary beyond words...

You pop the Eggos in the toaster and turn to look
at the screen.

                YOU
             (into phone)
That's what I mean: we got to accentuate
the positive, get this thing off dead
center, else we're never going to make
this fucking movie, let alone make it
this summer when the leaves are the
right color....

ON SCREEN
Close shots of dead mutilated bodies being heaved
onto a truck. Frozen corpses, black blood, open
eyes. Wooden soldiers working in slow motion,
picking up the mangled bodies and throwing them
like heavy sacks of coal.

ON you
Staring, still talking.

                YOU
             (into phone)
So what if Ted's got seven scripts to
read.... Have Jonathan call him and tell

him to read ours first. You gotta take
charge, Harry...

ON SCREEN

                    REPORTER (V.O.)
...these pictures courtesy of ITN News,
one of whose cameramen suffered
multiple...

                    YOU (CONTINUING, V.O.)
Tell him to say we'll send Kimberley
over and have her read it to him, out
loud.... Ted'll like Kimberley. Hell,
Dina'll like Kimberley...

Extreme close shots now of the dead bodies, a slow
series of static shots of frozen faces, eyes open,
contorted limbs, grotesque postures, silent,
unmoving.

                    YOU (CONTINUING, V.O.)
Kimberley knows how to spread joy up to
the max—

CLOSE ON
You. Still staring at the screen, you suddenly
stop talking. You look down and to the right.

                    REPORTER (V.O.)
...so now the long and painful process
of identifying...

Your P.O.V.:

CLOSE ON
Your daughter Sophie, six years old, dressed in a
white tee shirt with red lettering that says
"Don't Mess with Texas." She is staring intently
at the television screen filled with pictures of
dead bodies, shot after shot after shot of dead

bodies. She is transfixed, the same way we will later see her when she is staring at *Clarissa Explains It All* on Nickelodeon.

                                        CUT TO:

BLACK SCREEN. Sudden silence. Then the pristine eye and morphing VOICE, CAMERA exploring as before.

                    VOICE (V.O.)
     ...the information comes at night. The
     communications technology it picks is
     not the phone or the fax or the E-mail.
     It is the telex—so its teeth can
     chatter in your head.... The information
     is advertising a symposium of pain. Pain
     of all faiths and denominations. These
     are your little ones, these are your
     pretty ones. Become accustomed to their
     voices. They will grow louder, and more
     persistent, and more persuasive, until
     they're all there is.[4]

                                        CUT TO:

INT. BASEMENT OFFICE   NIGHT

CLOSE ON
A blue computer screen. The SOUND of typing on a keyboard. Letters appear on the screen: "Curriculum Vitae." The typing stops. The only sound is the hum of the computer fan and the hint of a television set somewhere upstairs, tuned to an *I Love Lucy* rerun.

You hunch over the keyboard, head jutted out toward the screen, staring at the words. Beside you on the wall are hundreds of scraps of paper, most white, some yellow and salmon and pink, some gray with age, a few Post-its and business cards and one photograph of you, a passport picture taken in the early 1970s, black plastic glasses, lots of dark hair freshly combed and matted, heavy eyes and jowls, no expression. A static face, awkward before the camera.

All the scraps of paper are filled with words, scribbles, doodles, names, numbers, addresses—a collage, random, timeless, making rapidly receding sense to one set of bifocaled eyes only, yet one jumbled measure of a life, of tentative reachings, markers of other times and other places when reaching still seemed possible.

You move in closer to the screen, your back hunched, shoulders held unnaturally high, as if you were driving a race car and leaning into the windscreen.

Your fingers type.

Words on the screen: "B-o-r-n:" Pause. "Y-e-s-t-e-r-d-a-y."

CUT TO:

BLACK SCREEN. Sudden silence. Then the pristine eye and morphing VOICE, CAMERA exploring as before.

> VOICE (V.O.)
> We might note the effect of speed in Baudrillard's own...style of discourse, in his quite deliberate use of generalizations not weighed down by qualifications. Why write a book when you can write an essay? Why write an essay when you can produce an aphorism? Why even bother with an aphorism when you can come up with a pun?[5]

CUT TO:

EXT. MONTE CARLO DAY
Moving aerial shot of the city during the Grand Prix, the Formula One cars tearing down the winding streets, crowds of people watching, mouths

open in apparent cheers, bodies stretched to see,
leaning in the direction of the race, as if sucked
along with the momentum, as if in a cartoon. A
helicopter crosses frame, turns sharply and dives
toward the race.

INT. HELICOPTER   DAY
Jonathan and the pilot in the front, eyes wide,
excited, laughing, looking eagerly at the crowded
spectacular landscape.

> PILOT
> (yelling)
> There, Jonathan! The leader, the
> Ferrari, in front of the casino!

And the helicopter plunges suddenly toward the
race, zooming in for a closer look, the G-force
tossing Jonathan back in his seat.

You are belted into the rear seat, frozen in
terror, holding on to a strap, eyes looking out
the window, transfixed and wide, unable not to
look.

CLOSE ON
Your face, eyes not blinking, forced to watch,
watching in spite of yourself, consumed with
fascination and with dread.

                                        CUT TO:

EXT. MONTE CARLO STREET DAY
A Formula One car races toward the wildly tracking
camera at incredible speed. Camera whips around
with the racer as it spins out of control and
another speeding car rams into it.

CLOSE ON
The driver's face, spinning and rolling, eyes wide
open, his mouth opening for a scream as we HEAR a
deafening CRASH and EXPLOSION.

                                        CUT TO:

BLACK SCREEN. Sudden silence. Then the pristine eye and morphing VOICE, CAMERA exploring as before.

> VOICE (V.O.)
> There is something faintly insane about belief, but conviction, which is redoubling of belief, is downright moronic. Conviction is only outdone in this regard by truly rampant imbecility.[6]

CUT TO:

INT. CARLTON HOTEL RESTAURANT NIGHT
CAMERA moves toward and around a round table, eight people talking, four men in tuxedos, four women in evening wear. Behind them, the lights of Cannes sparkle through a window, reflected in a calm sea of blue-black-silver. Hushed conversation, sparkling glasses and silverware, a spectacular floral centerpiece.

One of the men is the director Arthur Penn, at ease in his role as human centerpiece.

Another is the actor David Soul, Starsky from *Starsky and Hutch*, now a cabaret singer with a voice of silk, his tux California trendy, smoke-gray ruffled shirt, no tie.

Ultimately, CAMERA comes to rest on you, your shirt pinching your neck, beads of sweat on your brow. You are seated next to Tanya, a large woman with short hair and oversized earrings and black make-up, a television producer-reporter from CNN in Atlanta who rustles uncomfortably in her ill-fitting dress. She and you are drinking champagne.

> YOU
> (to Tanya)
> ...a picnoleptic moment—[7]

>   TANYA
> Picnoleptic?

>   YOU
> Picnoleptic. Paul Virilio defines it as
> that moment when the senses function,
> but they are closed to external
> impressions. You know, when you blank
> out for a second, or a minute, you don't
> really know how long, but when you snap
> out of it someone is talking to you and
> you have no idea what was said. You were
> receiving no information. World War
> Three could have happened and you missed
> it. That's a picnoleptic moment. Virilio
> says we can have hundreds of them during
> a day, most passing completely
> unnoticed.

>   TANYA
> Virilio?

>   YOU
> A French philosopher. He writes mostly
> about speed, the speed of information
> and what it's doing to us, how the
> faster we go, the more it seems like
> we're standing still.

>   TANYA
> You said you're a producer? Feature
> films? Do you have a movie in
> competition? An art film, maybe? You
> didn't do *Trainspotting*, did you, or
> another one of those pointless
> depressing downer films? You don't look
> like a producer to me. You look more
> like a lawyer or a philosopher or
> something.

>   YOU
> My life's a picnoleptic moment...

>   TANYA
> You wish.

You look down at your plate.

Your P.O.V.:
Neatly arranged food, colorful, seductive. What
looks like a fried mushroom, a bit of lobster,
cold baby asparagus, strategically placed splashes
of sauce, swirls of arranged color, seductive
beyond imagination, an rush of come-hither
delights.

CLOSE ON
You, eyeing the mushroom.

> TANYA (OFF SCREEN)
> Arthur, dear, I simply loved your film.
> Lou Gossett is a much better South
> African freedom fighter than Morgan
> Freeman or even Denzel. It's going to
> make an absolute—

CUT TO:

BLACK SCREEN. Sudden silence. Then the pristine
eye and morphing VOICE, CAMERA exploring as
before.

> VOICE (V.O.)
> Laundering money, laundering history,
> laundering memory by restoring an
> ambiguous virginity to them; laundering
> events, even laundering the libido,
> clearing its name by merrily attaching
> it to false objects of desire—launder,
> launder, launder everything black,
> illegal, apocryphal.... The whole of
> money is illegal, all memory is illegal,
> it has to be smuggled through....[8]

CUT TO:

Back on the plate of food. Your hand reaches into
frame and picks up the mushroom.

                    TANYA (OFF SCREEN)
                      (laughing)
          And *Inside*'s such a perfect title.
          Inside a South African prison, inside
          Lou's head. Your direction just sucks
          us—the audience, the world—right
          inside it all, the politics, the
          inhumanity, the evils of apartheid. And
          yet you give us hope...

                    ARTHUR PENN (OFF SCREEN)
          You're so sweet. And so perceptive to
          notice. I find southern Africa so
          compelling. I'm setting my next film
          there as well. Mozambique perhaps, or
          Angola. A black fado, an African *Black
          Orpheus*. Something poetical for a
          change. Portuguese is such a sad
          language, so filled with longing...

You take a bite of the mushroom, oil dripping down
your fingers. Still listening to Penn, Tanya
watches you out of the corner of her eye, as she
cuts hers with a knife and fork, slips a tiny bite
between her teeth.

You pop the whole thing in your mouth. A look of
shock, of amazement, of pleasant surprise, your
face coming alive, a positively delighted reaction
to an unexpected taste explosion.

                         YOU
                (food still in your mouth)
          This is wonderful! The mushroom, the
          glorious essence of it! The flavor's so
          intense. It tastes like, I don't know
          what! It tastes like, like France
          itself, exotic, vibrant, sensual,
          irresistible—
                        TANYA
          It's not a mushroom. It's fois gras.
          Duck liver or something. Goose, maybe.

Like something out of a Peter Greenaway
film. Undercooked and probably teeming
with microbes.

On you, frozen in mid-chew.

        ARTHUR PENN (OFF SCREEN)
...the misery of Mozambique, the agony
of Angola—

                           CUT TO:

BLACK SCREEN. Sudden silence. Then the pristine
eye and morphing VOICE, CAMERA exploring as
before.

          VOICE (V.O.)
True poetry is that which has lost all
the distinctive signs of poetry. If
poetry exists, it is anywhere but in
poetry.... So it is with philosophy. The
whole world has become philosophical....
There is no point questioning it as to
its ends; it is beyond ends. Nor as to
its cause; it knows only effects.... All
of philosophy and poetry come back to us
from places where we were no longer
expecting to find them.[9]

                           CUT TO:

INT. BEDROOM   NIGHT
Tangled in a sheet, you lie asleep in your bed,
your body unnaturally contorted and stiff, like
one of the corpses in the news report from Bosnia
but without obvious wounds and the black blood;
the flicker of television light dances around you,
a faint SOUND of VOICES coming from the set.

CLOSE ON
Your face, asleep, but not resting, a pained
expression, your neck at an odd angle, muscles

tight in preparation for a morning spasm. But you do not toss, nor move. For you movement in sleep, shifting from one contortion to another, has become a willful and conscious act, perhaps the only one left to you, this desperate quest for a possible position in which to pursue the unconscious.

CLOSE ON
The unwatched TV. Bernard Kalb is talking to Tanya. The sound is low, but audible now.

> BERNIE
> So Woody Harrelson didn't mind talking to the press? The bad reviews of Cimino's film didn't send him running for cover? I've heard he can become quite violent with reporters—

> TANYA
> The Cannes festival is such an unreal world, Bernie. Anything can happen. Right now it all seems to me like a carnival dream. Was I really there only a week ago, amid the glamour and the stars, me, interviewing Dustin Hoffman, dancing with Arthur Penn, flirting with Woody? Or was it all just another picnoleptic moment?

On you, your eyes still closed, your hand reaching up and grabbing your neck, the pain so common you sleep through it.

CUT TO:

BLACK SCREEN. Sudden silence. Then the pristine eye and morphing VOICE, CAMERA exploring as before.

> VOICE (V.O.)
> Who was said to be the last man to have read everything? Coleridge. Hazlitt.

Gibbon. Coleridge: it was Coleridge. Two
hundred years on, nobody had read a
millionth of everything, and the
fraction was getting smaller every day.
And every new book held less and less of
the whole.[10]

                                      CUT TO:

EXT. PARK   DAY
You stand awkwardly next to John, a tall, athletic
mathematician. You and he are saying nothing,
looking out. The SOUND of children playing.

Your P.O.V.:
Two two-year-old kids, Lily and Johnny, your
daughter and John's son, are attempting to climb a
metal jungle gym. The potential for a fall, a
banged head, chipped teeth, broken limb is very
real and is captured in your face.

                    JOHN
        Found a job yet?

You and John don't look at each other as you talk,
both of you watching the kids as Johnny creeps
ahead of Lily, both ascending higher and higher.

                    YOU
        I made a short list again, somewhere,
        Augusta, Georgia, I think, some
        community college. But I won't get it.

                    JOHN
        Why not?

                    YOU
        Same reason. Too white, too male, too
        old.

                    JOHN
        What?

                    YOU
    Irony, John. I'm being ironical.
    Cloaking myself in protective folds of
    Baudrillardian irony.

                    JOHN
    Surely you're not saying—

                                        CUT TO:

    BLACK SCREEN. Sudden silence. Then the pristine
    eye and morphing VOICE, CAMERA exploring as
    before.

                    VOICE (V.O.)
    The next day it was his turn: [he]
    turned forty. Turned is right. Like a
    half-cooked steak, like a wired cop,
    like an old leaf, like milk, he
    turned.[11]

                                        CUT TO:

    Back on John and you.

                    JOHN
    —that being old, white, and male—

                    YOU
    They'll look at me like I'm petrified, a
    grumpy old Walter Matthau of a guy who
    only reads from left to right, a
    patriarchal relic best left in a nursing
    home, the real museums of our age. Or
    else they'll hate my work. They won't
    "understand" it, not understanding that
    understanding is just another monumental
    un-understand-able.

    Your P.O.V.:
    The children. Lily loses her footing and starts to
    fall, but catches herself, barely and at the last

minute, and finally regains her foothold, high on
the hard metal bars. She seems unconcerned.

                    JOHN
        You really believe that, that they'll
        hate your work?

                    YOU
        I do autoethnography. Most of the time I
        hate it.

                                        CUT TO:

BLACK SCREEN. Sudden silence. Then the pristine
eye and morphing VOICE, CAMERA exploring as
before.

                    VOICE (V.O.)
        What is being destroyed more quickly
        than the ozone layer is the subtle layer
        of irony that protects us from the
        radiation of stupidity.... We are
        secreting information at such a rate
        that it is polluting the higher layers
        of the mental atmosphere with its
        non-degradable waste, gradually
        destroying the kind of atmospheric
        girdle which protects us from our
        secrets....[12]

                                        CUT TO:

Your P.O.V.:
Lily climbs higher, toward Johnny who is now at
the top of the jungle gym.

                    JOHN
        Autoethnography? What's that mean? You
        hang around used car lots taking notes?

                    YOU
        I could, John, but I don't. What I work
        at is corralling my fractured ironical

postmodern selves through writing. Only
all I ever produce is a disjointed
sequence of senseless shards that
superficially reflect my sundry
shattered and shattering subjectivities,
not to be too alliterative about it all.
Paralysis, atrophy, reification,
marginalization, pain, dread. Those
words mean anything to you, John?

John looks at you. Your eyes are still on Lily.
John shakes his head.

                    JOHN
Thank God I'm in the math department.

Lily slips again, barely catching herself again.

                    YOU
          (lurching toward Lily)
Thank God I'm not.

You grab Lily, lifting her off the metal bars. She
starts to CRY, fights you, kicking, wanting to get
out of your arms and back on the metal bars.

Lily SCREAMING at the top of her lungs, you
clinging to her, not letting her go.

                    JOHN
You should let her fall sometimes. How
else is she going to learn?

On you, your face red with anger, frustration,
Lily still SCREAMING in your arms, scrambling to
free herself from your grip. Your mouth opens and
you SCREAM at her, with her.

                                        CUT TO:

BLACK SCREEN. Sudden silence. Then the pristine
eye and morphing VOICE, CAMERA exploring as
before.

                         VOICE (V.O.)
        [He] stood there naked, looking at the
        bared sheet, its crenellations, its damp
        glow. Every morning we leave more in the
        bed: certainty, vigor, past loves. And
        hair, and skin: dead cells. This ancient
        detritus was nonetheless one move ahead
        of you, making its own humorless
        arrangements to rejoin the cosmos.[13]

                                              CUT TO:

        INT. CHILDREN'S BEDROOM   NIGHT
        A single bed. Sophie and Lily, the two daughters,
        are sleeping entwined, sweet faces, almost naked
        bodies, a peaceful quiet. They move gently in
        sleep, taking easy breaths, limbs flopping
        unconsciously, softly, naturally, smooth young
        skin, cool and content in the refracted moonlight.
        On you standing in the doorway, staring. A tear
        escapes your unblinking eyes. You wipe it away
        with a finger as you continue to stare, unable to
        move, frozen, transfixed.
                                              CUT TO:

        BLACK SCREEN. Sudden silence. Then the pristine
        eye and morphing VOICE, CAMERA exploring as
        before.

                         VOICE (V.O.)
        Why do men [cry in the night]? Because
        of fights and feats and marathon
        preferment, because they want their
        mothers, because they are blind in
        time...because of all that men have
        done. Because they can't be happy or sad
        anymore—only smashed or nuts. And
        because they don't know how to do it
        when they are awake. And then there is
        the information, which comes at night.[14]

                                              CUT TO:

INT. BASEMENT OFFICE   DAY
Close on the computer screen. Netscape. The
AltaVista search engine. The SOUND of typing, the
CLACK of a keyboard. The words "Dina Merrill" go
into the search block.

>   YOU (OFF SCREEN)
>   · (on phone)
>   ...saw it on the news last night, Harry.
>   Dan Rather, not *Inside Edition*, so it
>   has to be true, right? Scientists have
>   discovered that prolonged stress causes
>   brain shrinkage and memory loss in
>   rats...

On the screen, the pointer clicks on "Search," and
a new page listing various options appears.
Scrolling fast, the mouse clicks on one of the
links, then another link.

>   YOU (OFF SCREEN)
>   (on phone)
>   ...here it is, just like I thought. She
>   was in *Caddyshack II* as well. Dina and
>   Ted must have met there. She's worth
>   hundreds of millions, Harry, heir to a
>   manufacturing fortune, and she's working
>   with a bunch of rodents—cyborg,
>   mechanical, two-legged—

Another click and another link appears, a photo
downloads, Dina Merrill, beautiful but blurred as
the pixels accumulate and clarity approaches.

>   YOU (OFF SCREEN)
>   (on phone)
>   ...I know, Harry...I felt it in Cannes.
>   Jonathan's not going to put up a
>   dime.... And he's not going to get Ted
>   and Dina to invest, either. We should

have seen it, Harry, you know. All he
wanted to do was hang out at Cannes, go
to Dina's party, have lunch with
Patricia Arquette, buzz the Grand Prix
in that fucking helicopter. We should
have read the signs. Instead, we chose
to accentuate the positive and ended up
messing with Mr. In Between. No money,
no movie, not this year, not any year.
More wasted time, more shattered dreams,
too much of everything painful, Harry. I
can feel those neurons shrinking behind
my very eyes, shriveling, performing a
rat-like disappearance...

On the screen, another few CLICKS and links lead
to a colorful screen with the headline "Welcome to
the Post-Modernity Project's Home Page. The
University of Virginia."

                YOU (OFF SCREEN)
                  (on phone)
What am I going to do? I don't know.
Hibernate, maybe. Watch TV. Wait till
spring. Take a teaching job in Georgia,
if I can get it. Forget about this damn
business, this outrageously seductive
business you keep dragging me back to
with promises of fame and fortune. And
you, Harry, you old codger, what about
you?

                                    CUT TO:

BLACK SCREEN. Sudden silence. Then the pristine
eye and morphing VOICE, CAMERA exploring as
before.

                  VOICE (V.O.)
By his own admission, Descartes only
thought for two or three minutes a day.

The rest of the time, he went riding, he
lived. What are we to make of these
modern thinkers, then, who think
fourteen hours a day?[15]

INT. PROFESSOR'S OFFICE   DAY
A typical professor's office at a large midwestern
university, filled with shelves of books along
every wall. Even the window is mostly hidden
behind books, magazines, papers. The desk is
covered with other precarious piles of papers,
a partially visible computer screen off to the
right, its Monet screen saver rotating silently,
happily.

You can barely see the PROFESSOR between the
stacks of paper.

> PROFESSOR
> I hear you went to the Cannes Film
> Festival.

> YOU
> A small consulting job that didn't pan
> out. But I did get to have lunch with
> Dina Merrill. And dinner with Arthur
> Penn. I saw *Trainspotting* and watched
> the Grand Prix from a helicopter.

> PROFESSOR
> And so?

> YOU
> And so? And so nothing.

CUT TO:

BLACK SCREEN. Sudden silence. Then the pristine
eye and morphing VOICE, CAMERA exploring as
before.

> VOICE (V.O.)
> Another Crash lies in wait for us, that
> of cultural overproduction.... Even now,

unbridled creativity exceeds our
capacity to absorb it....[16]

CUT TO:

Back on the Professor and you.

You watch as the Professor, still partially hidden
behind a stack of journals, leafs quickly through
your term paper. His hand and eye are practiced,
confident, in command.

                PROFESSOR
I must say I found this extremely
irritating. You don't show any evidence
of scholarship at all. All these random
unrelated unexplained quotes, and in the
footnotes, yet. Confessional,
narcissistic, maddeningly elliptical...

                YOU
Elliptical?

                PROFESSOR
What's your point? And even if I could
figure that out, even if you gave me
enough information so I could figure it
out, so what? Who cares? Where's the
positive move? Where's the context, the
politics, the lit review? What's the
scholarly significance of a girl named
Trix, for God's sake? If you want to do
a "mystory," autoethnography, that's
fine. But for me, it's not cultural
studies. Sorry if that's narrow-minded,
but, well, that's just the way it is.

The Professor looks at you, now slouched in your
chair.

On the Professor, continuing:

                PROFESSOR
Just once I'd like to see some evidence
of intellectual rigor.

A long pause.

                    YOU
     Rigor? Isn't that something usually
     associated with mortis?

                                        CUT TO:

BLACK SCREEN. Sudden silence. Then the pristine
eye and morphing VOICE, CAMERA exploring as
before.

                  VOICE (V.O.)
     Why write a book when you can write an
     essay? Why write an essay when you can
     produce an aphorism? Why even bother
     with an aphorism when you can come up
     with a pun?[17]

                                        CUT TO:

Back on the Professor and you.

                  PROFESSOR
     Please don't make puns. I hate puns.
     Don't add to the clutter with puns.
     Don't add to the pain.

                    YOU
     I don't add. I subtract. I'm
     elliptical...

The Professor glares at you. You avert your eyes.

                                        CUT TO:

BLACK SCREEN. Sudden silence. Then the pristine
eye and morphing VOICE, CAMERA exploring as
before.

                  VOICE (V.O.)
     The excess of information, of faxing, of
     interfacing gives us infarction. After
     the infarction comes the artefact and

the prosthesis. After the artefact, the
lapsus and the collapse....[18]

CUT TO:

INT. LIVING ROOM   DAY
On the television set tuned to Nickelodeon. The
opening credit sequence of *Clarissa Explains It
All*, the music and the singing—no words, just "Na
Na Na" sounds, jaunty rhythmic utterances with
just a hint of melody.

On Sophie, watching, mesmerized, singing "Na Na
Na" in sync with the television.

On you, lying on a large sofa, your head propped
up with pillows, unnaturally perpendicular to your
horizontal body, your hair an uncombed mess, your
clothes stained and unironed, a *New Yorker* open
and wrinkled on your chest, your arm dangling limp
over the sofa's edge.

Piled up around you are other magazines, books,
Xeroxed readings from academic journals, a jungle
of printed material. Just out of reach on the
floor is a tattered copy of Larry Grossberg's
book, *We Gotta Get Out of This Place*, with a
fringe of ripped yellow Post-its sticking out from
between its pages. Stamped on the back of the book
are the words "JUST SAY YES."

Again, your stillness and the angle of your head
and limbs bring back visions of rigor mortis. But
you in your daze, like Sophie in her enthusiasm,
are merely watching television, you staring
blankly, lips dry, eyes bloodshot, encircled by
graying bags of limp flesh. You do not sing along.

The doorbell RINGS. You get up and go to the front
door, stumbling through the printed materials at
your feet, kicking over a large bottle of Gatorade
in the process.

A woman stands there at the threshold, awkwardly.
She is tall, thin, bent, shy, in her late sixties,

with a soft voice and large gray eyes, magnified
to unnatural size by thick glasses. You talk to
her through the screen door.

                    YOU
     Hi, Grace.

                    GRACE
     I hope I'm not disturbing your supper. I
     purposely didn't come during the news.

                    YOU
     No. Just watching *Clarissa Explains It
     All*, reading, trying to catch up...

                    GRACE
     Bill and I are going away for the
     weekend. Could you possibly collect the
     papers and see to the mail? We'll be
     back Monday or Tuesday.

                    YOU
     Sure.

                    GRACE
     If you need us, we'll be at the Holiday
     Inn in Angola. I've written down the
     number.

She slips you a tiny scrap of paper through a
crack in the door.

                    YOU
     Angola? You're going to Angola for the
     weekend?

                    GRACE
     Bill's mother—she'll be ninety-five in
     October—is in a nursing home there. We
     haven't seen her since she was admitted.
     She's had a fall, slipped and fell,
     Bill's concerned—

                                        CUT TO:

BLACK SCREEN. Sudden silence. Then the pristine eye and morphing VOICE, CAMERA exploring as before.

                    VOICE (V.O.)
Cipher, do not decipher. Work over the illusion. Create illusion to create an event. Make enigmatic what is clear, render unintelligible what is only too intelligible, make the event itself unreadable. Accentuate the false transparency of the world.... The absolute rule is to give back more than you were given. Never less, always more. The absolute rule...is to give back the world as it was given to us—unintelligible. And if possible to render it a little more unintelligible.[19]

                                        CUT TO:

Back on you and Grace, at the door.

                    YOU
In Angola? Are you sure? Angola?

                SOPHIE (OFF SCREEN)
                    (yelling)
Who is it? Is it Grace?

                    YOU
                (to Sophie)
Yes, it's Grace. She's going to Africa for the weekend.

                    GRACE
Angola, Indiana. It's about a three-and-a-half-hour drive from here. It's not in Africa. It's in Indiana. Don't be silly. My lord, Africa.

<pre>
                        YOU
                     (pause)
      Oh... Sounds like Africa, though.
      Angola. Portuguese *fados* and the like,
      in Africa. Africa's more exotic than
      Indiana, more elementary.... I'd rather
      go to Africa any day.... I'd rather
      shoot my movie in Africa any day...
</pre>

Sophie appears at your side.

<pre>
                      SOPHIE
      Grace, when you're in Africa, are you
      going to see any dead people?
</pre>

CUT TO:

BLACK SCREEN. Sudden silence. Then the pristine
eye and morphing VOICE, CAMERA exploring as
before.

<pre>
                    VOICE (V.O.)
      ...with acceleration, to travel is like
      filming, not so much producing images as
      new mnemonic traces, unlikely,
      supernatural. In such a context death
      itself can no longer be felt as mortal;
      it becomes...a simple technical
      accident, the final separation of the
      sound from the picture track.[20]
</pre>

CAMERA moves through the eye into a field of
black.

DISSOLVE TO:

INT. OFFICE   NIGHT

CLOSE UP of COMPUTER SCREEN, blank except for a
slowly blinking cursor.

On you sitting in the darkness, starting to type
at your computer. The CLACK of keys.

ZOOM IN over your shoulder into the screen until
the picture area fills the frame. Words appear on
the screen as you type them:

---

even my picnolepic moments are no longer my own,
filled as they have become with the voices of
intruders...and so...so what?...so what...so
where...so who...so when...so how...so long...so
so...ad/verbs...pre/positions...so
what...whatever...see georgio agamben on
whatever... whatever...so what?...

SUDDEN SILENCE

But this time no eye, only the computer screen,
with the typing continuing. The VOICE is still the
same, though, a morphing succession of many
voices.
                    VOICE (V.O.)
    The coming being is whatever being...not
    "being, it does not matter which," but
    rather "being such that it always
    matters."... Thus, whatever singularity
    (the Lovable) is never the intelligence
    of some thing, of this or that quality
    or essence, but the intelligence of an
    intelligibility....

    The movement...that transports the
    object not toward another thing or
    another place, but toward its own
    taking-place—toward the Idea....[21]

    Whatever singularity, which wants to
    appropriate belonging itself, its own
    being-in-language, and thus rejects all
    identity and every condition of
    belonging, is the principal enemy of the
    State. Wherever these singularities
    peacefully demonstrate their being in
    common there will be Tiananmen, and,

```
sooner or later, the tanks will
appear.²²
```

```
Typing continues, in silence on the screen:
```

```
whatever...two questions occur to me...what would
this look like filmed...what would the soundtrack
be...whatever
```

```
And the screen slowly fills with dots, pushing the
words higher and higher until they disappear,
leaving only the dots, an excess of ellipses...
```

```
FADE OUT
```

Notes

1. David Shields, "Why We Live at the Movies," *Utne Reader* (March/April 1994), p. 170.

2. Martin Amis, *The Information* (New York: Harmony Books, 1995), p. 4.

3. Shields, "Why We Live at the Movies," p. 170.

4. Amis, *The Information*, p. 340.

5. Ackbar Abbas, "Disappearance and Fascination: The Baudrillardian Obscenario," in *The Provocation of Jean Baudrillard*, Ackbar Abbas, ed. (Hong Kong: Twilight, 1990), p. 71.

6. Jean Baudrillard, *Cool Memories II*, Chris Turner, trans. (Durham, NC: Duke University Press, 1996), p. 15.

7. See Paul Virilio, *The Aesthetics of Disappearance* (New York: Semiotext(e), 1991), pp. 9–10.

8. Ibid., pp. 54–55.

9. Baudrillard, *Cool Memories II*, p. 65.

10. Amis, *The Information*, p. 178.

11. Ibid., p. 26.

12. Baudrillard, *Cool Memories II*, p. 34.

13. Amis, *The Information*, p. 145.

14. Ibid., p. 25.

15. Baudrillard, *Cool Memories II*, p. 25.

16. Ibid., p. 49.

17. Abbas, "Disappearance and Fascination," p. 71.

18. Ibid., p. 37.

19. Jean Baudrillard, *The Perfect Crime*, Chris Turner, trans. (London and New York: Verso, 1996), p. 104.

20. Virilio, *The Aesthetics of Disappearance*, p. 60.

21. Giorgio Agamben, *The Coming Community*, Michael Hardt, trans. (Minneapolis: University of Minnesota Press, 1993), pp. 2–3.

22. Ibid., pp. 86–87.

If I have said so little, almost nothing, it is out of desperate caution: I distrust every word and every ear.

—Helene Cixous, *Helene Cixous Reader*

Closures need not close off; they can be doors opening onto other closures and functioning as ongoing passages to elsewhere (-within-here). Like a throw of the dice, each opening is also a closing, for each work generates its own laws and limits, each has its specific condition and deals with a specific context. The closure here, however, is a way of letting go rather than sealing it off....

—Trinh Minh-ha, *When the Moon Waxes Red*

Epilogue: Desire

"I think there are dreams that can kill you. . . . More than people, or disease, or time."

—Arturo Perez-Reverte, *The Queen of the South*

```
FADE IN:

NEW MILLENNIUM
```

An African American student walks into my class late. He apologizes, good-natured sarcasm in his voice, and sits in the back row, bright-eyed and cocky, the only black student in the class. My first class. New semester, new way of life, late in life. Teaching. After class, he comes up to me, introduces himself. "My name is Hadjii." I try profiling. Drug dealer. Ex-marine, maybe. "Here," he says. "Read this." I look at it. An episode of *Seinfeld* by Hadjii. "Just read it," he says.

And I do, with him sitting there watching me. And it's brilliant, the tone just right, the dialogue perfect New York Jewish, the situations fresh, imaginative—Larry David couldn't have done it better. "I watch a lot of TV," Hadjii says. "You are a natural," I tell him. They are few and far between. The ear, the gut, the ease with written language. Hadjii. He smiles. "Trust me," he says with a smile, "you're right."

I begin working with him. I tell him that he shouldn't be writing *Seinfeld*. He should be writing a *Seinfeld*-like piece based on his own life. So he does, tentatively at first, worried about

167

the language. ("Can I use four-letter words? I've never written them down before"), worried about what his friends and family will think when they see themselves in print and on the screen as comic characters barely disguised. I tell him it's okay. He's a writer. He has to write what he knows, what he feels, capturing his own lived experience. I use the term "lived experience," which Norman Denzin taught me to say, and I am conscious of its weight the moment it passes my lips. But it doesn't keep me from quoting Trinh Minh-ha to him. "Writing is above all releasing oneself from external censorship. . . . Words . . . close to life expose. They share with the readers an intimacy that demands an equal laying bare and commitment on their part" (Trinh 1991, p. 130). "Uh huh," he says. "Here," I say, "take the book." "Ummm, well," he says, declining, "I don't read much." Later, he says, "I know you think I don't listen, but I hear everything. I mean I hear what you're saying. I take your points. I just don't read. It's better that way. Trust me."

Another student. Another natural writer, this one white, strawberry blonde even. I tell her that her screenplay, also lovely, reminds me of Tennessee Williams. She says, "Tennessee who?" Guy Maddin, the brilliant Winnipegger director of *The Saddest Music in the World*, tells me at Roger Ebert's Overlooked Film Festival, "I never had much interest in movies, hardly ever watched them. When I got to be about thirty, I simply felt the urge to make a movie, so I did." And Miranda July, first-time director of *Me and You and Everyone We Know*, follows up: "I never watched movies either. I just knew this story would be best as a movie, not a novel or a performance piece, so I wrote it as a movie and made it." Hadjii: "If I do watch movies, they are always bad ones, only bad black ones nobody ever heard of. *Casablacka*, stuff like that. I learn what not to do from bad movies. What to do, that just comes naturally to me."

I wonder if I have discovered something worth writing about/thinking about. Anecdotal evidence that not working within a discursive formation (to excavate another phrase from my theoretical past), not being schooled in the canon, not having worked in a video store and seen every movie ever made (e.g., as Quentin Tarantino did), could herald a good thing. Such disinterest in "the way things have always been done," in the history of the medium, might, against all odds and conventional wisdom, produce original cinematic works that surprise and astound—movies that are filled with a sense of humanity missing from most Hollywood fare, that give us voices that touch the soul, that know nothing about reified cinematic structural mechanics, that are closer (as Trinh says) to life. I wonder: Are we entering an age of new primitives, whose nascent sophistication lies in the only place it should—the human heart?

Hadjii writes a feature-length screenplay rooted in his life (i.e., "lived experience"), a coming-of-age story about a black college student named Scottie, who comes from a strong ethnic background, a young man from the deep South who messes with drugs, alcohol, and sex while still embracing family and church, a kid who passes triumphantly in multiple worlds, who moves with ease and grace among them, until a girl comes into his life and a preacher catches his ear, and he decides to take a long hard look at where he is and where he's going. All of this with a deft, gut-splitting comic touch and, as Bill Keys, one of the few African American independent film executives, says, "the blackest sensibility I've ever seen on the page." I read it and love it, and I suggest its title from one of the preacher's sermons: *Somebodies*.

And so we shoot the film, over three weeks, with thirty-five thousand dollars cash, a digital video camera, actors from comedy clubs in black Atlanta, a sixty-five-year-old Iraqi cameraman from Britain, and an inexperienced crew of former students that dwindles to a core of six or so as the fourteen-hour days quickly take their toll. Hadjii stars, directs, motivates, and entertains. It is a happy, if exhausted, set. Nothing out of the ordinary in this digital age, when making a movie is as easy as painting a picture or writing a poem. Yet for me, the producer, it is something other. It takes me back to another time, another place, in Africa, when I watched Zulus disappear into the night on that remote movie location and could no longer find words for what I felt—indeed, when I found myself with no need to express myself, no need for desire, no need for anything beyond what joined me to that frozen moment, for I was a part of all that I ever longed for; I was somehow satiated, wanting nothing, except for it to last forever.

Standing there now, over thirty years later, in a klieg-lit kitchen in Athens, Georgia, within the bustle of actors and crew, answering urgent questions about wardrobe and line delivery, I know I am home; I have found my way out of and into the wilderness.

In Cannes, a few months after, during the time of festival, I show a rough cut of the film to Paul Cox, the Dutch Australian director of over thirty films, all of which champion the human spirit, engaging in one way or another love and death and the healing agony of human touch. He likes *Somebodies*, and says Hadjii did a magnificent job for a first-time director. He tells me that I have found a rare talent and nurtured it, exactly what a producer is supposed to do. And then we talk about the mystery of making movies as an object of desire, the dream that seduces us, a seduction that becomes an obsession. And for me, an obsession for decades laced with a consuming dread that leaves me numb, confounded, and physically and emotionally atrophied—my life as a flame once touched, now only watched, feared from afar. And yet, and yet, there is still that desire, a perceived purity in the soul, a strange stain of clarity, that translates into a longing, an ache, a need—what is it about making movies, what is it about that desire that always resurfaces, what is it about the hunger that refuses to die?

Paul Cox smokes a cigar in the long Riviera twilight. In the streets below the balcony, mad people with badges around their necks rush to screenings and receptions and press conferences, hurrying, afraid they might miss something in the crammed twelve days of the Cannes Film Festival. Each one, in his or her own way, is a professional member of the international film community—if such a thing actually exists, as if making movies could ever be a profession, let alone a call to anything approaching Agamben's coming community. Paul pays the urgent horde no mind, nursing his cigar back to life. "Instead of seeing a psychiatrist, I make films." He talks to me because he and I have a similar sensibility—a certain self-reflexivity with regard to film, making movies, and the human condition. "I use film to give form and shape to illusions and dreams, to create a more solid reality than the daily reality I have to live with." I realize he is talking less about the content of his films and much more about the process of making them, about being lost (as I was, first in Africa, then with Hadjii in Georgia, so many years later) in the moments of making. "I arrest time, something adds up." It is that "something" that neither of us can clearly see, but we know it, when it is with us, during the making of movies. "And in that process, I might touch another human soul in passing. Meet fellow travelers. Feel less alone."

He rolls the ash off the end of his cigar. Yes, I think, but for me it is more self-centered. I desire it to live, to ignite my senses, to feel alive. It is probably the same for him, but it is also something else. Perhaps, because he has seen more of the horrors of the world than I have, in World War II Holland, and throughout Southeast Asia and India and the Middle East in times of civil war and other disasters, Paul Cox understands it more autoethnographically, more generously, unlike the way I do with my self-obsessions, in my relentless conceit. Unlike me, he is political. He says, "I need to escape from the collective insanity that is all around us. I need to escape and find other grounds, otherwise I would cease to exist." He pauses and says quietly, "I make films because I don't understand that Bush was reelected on a moral vote instead of going to jail." Maybe, I think.

Maybe Paul finds in the process of making films a world free of ambiguity and contradiction and terror, a short escape, a few weeks in a closed universe of his making where, grounded among fellow travelers, he can ensure that everything somehow touches the heart with remarkable tenderness. But it is more fundamental than the security found in being able to control a crew, actors, a story, an environment. It comes back, finally, as everything does, to desire. And to desire achieved, and in that achieving, finding and sustaining, for lack of another word, what Helene Cixous calls *joissance*, "which can be defined as a virtually metaphysical fulfillment of desire that goes far beyond [mere] satisfaction.... [It is a] fusion of the erotic, the mystical, and the political" (Gilbert 1986, p. xvii).

Paul then quotes Vaslav Nijinsky: "You will understand me when you see me dance."

The swirl of theory. Teasing me out of shape. I take a deep breath. Paul looks tired, ashen, staring at the people in the street below. His cigar forgotten in an ashtray, he looks suddenly alone. Two old men, suddenly alone. Are those tears in his eyes? I feel myself no longer there.

How did I get to a fusion of erotic, mystical, political? Or a linkage of seduction, obsession, dread, desire? Do these words mean anything? Have I shown you, in these hundreds of pages, things you haven't already seen, told you anything you didn't already know? I sense a terrible loss. Do I have enough time left? Dare I dream again?

Selected Bibliography

Abbas, A. (1990). Disappearance and fascination: The Baudrillardian obscenario. In A. Abbas (ed.), *The provocation of Jean Baudrillard* (pp. 68–93). Hong Kong: Twilight.

Agamben, G. (1993). *The coming community*. (M. Hardt, trans.). Minneapolis: University of Minnesota Press.

Ahmad, A. (1992). *In theory: Classes, nations, literatures*. London and New York: Verso.

Amis, M. (1995). *The information*. New York: Harmony Books.

Anderson, B. (1983). *Imagined communities*. London and New York: Verso.

Anzaldúa, G. (1999). *Borderlands/La frontera: The new mestiza*. San Francisco: Aunt Lute Books.

Arendt, H. (1968). Introduction. In W. Benjamin, *Illuminations* (pp. 1–59). New York: Schocken Books.

Bakhtin, M. M. (1986). *Speech genres and other late essays*. (V. W. McGee, trans.). Austin: University of Texas Press.

Barthes R. (1982). *A Barthes reader*. (S. Sontag, ed.). New York: Hill and Wang.

Baudelaire, C. (1962). *The flowers of evil*. (M. Mathews and J. Mathews, eds.). New York: New Directions.

———. (1964). *The painter of modern life and other essays*. (J. Mayne, ed. and trans.). London: Phaidon.

Baudrillard, J. (1983a). *In the shadow of the silent majorities*. New York: Semiotext(e).

———. (1983b). *Simulations*. New York: Semiotext(e).

———. (1989). The anorexic ruins. (D. Antal, trans.). In D. Kampfer and C. Wulf (eds.), *Looking back on the end of the world* (pp. 31–45). New York: Semiotext(e).

———. (1988). *Selected writings, edited and introduced by Mark Poster.* Stanford, CA: Stanford University Press.

———. (1996). *Cool memories II.* (C. Turner, trans.). Durham, NC: Duke University Press.

———. (1996). *The perfect crime.* London and New York: Verso.

———. (1997). *Fragments: Cool memories III, 1991–95.* London and New York: Verso.

Bauman, Z. (1997). *Postmodernity and its discontents.* New York: New York University Press.

Benjamin, W. (1968). *Illuminations.* (H. Arendt, ed.). New York: Schocken Books.

———. (1996). *Selected writings, volume 1.* Cambridge, MA: Belknap Press of Harvard University.

———. (1999). *The Arcades Project.* (H. Eiland and K. McLaughlin, trans.). Cambridge, MA: Belknap Press of Harvard University.

Best, S., and D. Kellner. (1991). *Postmodern theory.* New York: Guilford Press.

Bhabha, H. K. (1994). *The location of culture.* New York and London: Routledge.

Boon, J. (1991). Why museums make me sad. In I. Karp and S. Levine (eds.), *Exhibiting cultures: The poetics and politics of museum display* (pp. 255–278). Washington and London: Smithsonian Institute.

Borsboom, A. (1988). The savage in European social thought: A prelude to the conceptualization of the divergent peoples and cultures of Australia and Oceania. *Bijdragen, 144,* 419–432.

Bourdieu, P. (1984). *Distinction: A social critique of the judgement of taste* (R. Nice, trans.). London: Routledge & Kegan Paul.

Bruner, E. M. (1989). Tourism, creativity, and authenticity. *Studies in Symbolic Interaction, 10,* 109–114.

Buchan, J. (1916). *Greenmantle.* London: Hodder and Stoughton.

Buck-Morss, S. (1989). *The dialectics of seeing: Walter Benjamin and the Arcades Project.* Cambridge, MA, and London: MIT Press.

Calvino, I. (1981). *If on a winter's night a traveler.* New York: Harcourt Brace & Company.

Carey, J. W. (1988). *Communication as culture.* Boston: Unwin Hyman.

Carver, R. (1989a). *Fires.* New York: Vintage Contemporaries.

———. (1989b). *What we talk about when we talk about love.* New York: Vintage Contemporaries.

Chang, H. (1993). Postmodern communities: The politics of oscillation. *Postmodern Culture, 4*, paras. 1–54.

Chatterjee, P. (1986). *Nationalist thought and the colonial world.* Minneapolis: University of Minnesota Press.

Chow, R. (1991). *Woman and Chinese modernity: The politics of reading between west and east.* Minneapolis: University of Minnesota Press.

———. (1993). *Writing diaspora.* Bloomington: University of Indiana Press.

Cixous, H. (1994). *The Helene Cixous reader.* (S. Sellers, ed.). New York and London: Routledge.

Clifford, J. (1992). Traveling cultures. In L. Grossberg, C. Nelson, and P. Treichler (eds.), *Cultural Studies* (pp. 96–116). New York and London: Routledge.

Clough, P. T. (1992). *The end(s) of ethnography.* London: Sage.

———. (1994). *Feminist thought.* Cambridge, MA, and Oxford, UK: Blackwell.

de Certeau, M. (1984). *The practice of everyday life.* Berkeley: University of California Press.

Deleuze, G. (1985). Mediators. In J. Cray and S. Kwinter (eds.), *Zone 6: Incorporations* (pp. 268–280). New York: Urzone.

Denzin, N. K. (1991). *Images of postmodern society: Social theory and contemporary cinema.* London: Sage.

———. (1992). *Symbolic interactionism and cultural studies: The politics of interpretation.* Cambridge, MA, and Oxford, UK: Blackwell.

———. (1994). Evaluating qualitative research in the poststructural moment: The lessons James Joyce teaches us. *Qualitative Studies in Education, 7,* 295–308.

———. (1997). *Interpretive ethnography: Ethnographic practices for the 21st century.* Thousand Oaks, CA, and London: Sage.

Denzin, N. K., and Y. Lincoln (1994). *Handbook of qualitative research.* Thousand Oaks, CA, and London: Sage.

Derrida, J. (1976). *Of grammatology.* (G. Spivak, trans.). Baltimore: Johns Hopkins University Press.

Eco, U. (1973). *Travels in hyperreality.* San Diego: Harcourt Brace Jovanovich.

Ellul, J. (1965). *Propaganda.* New York: Vintage Books.

Featherstone, M. (1991). *Consumer culture & postmodernism.* London: Sage.

Foucault, M. (1977). *Language/counter-memory/practice.* (D. F. Bouchard, ed., D. F. Bouchard and S. Simon, trans.). Ithaca, NY: Cornell University Press.

————. (1978). *The history of sexuality: An introduction, volume 1.* New York: Random House.

————. (1984). *The Foucault reader.* (P. Rabinow, ed.). New York: Pantheon Books

Freud, S. (1979). From the history of an infantile neurosis (the "Wolf Man"). In A. Richards and J. Strachey (eds.), *Pelican Freud Library 9* (J. Strachey, trans.). Harmondsworth, UK: Penguin.

Gamson, J. (1994). *Claims to fame: Celebrity in contemporary America.* Berkeley: University of California Press.

Gilbert, S. M. (1986). Introduction. In Helene Cixous and Catherine Clement, *The Newly Born Woman* (B. Wing, trans.). Minneapolis: University of Minnesota Press.

Gilroy, P. (1987). *There ain't no black in the union jack.* Chicago: University of Chicago Press.

Grossberg, L. (1992). *We gotta get out of this place.* New York and London: Routledge.

Habermas, J. (1992). *The structural transformation of the public sphere.* Cambridge, MA: MIT Press.

Hall, S. (1990). The emergence of cultural studies and the crisis of the humanities. *October, 53,* 11–90.

Hawkes, T. (1977). *Structuralism and semiotics.* Berkeley: University of California Press.

Hebdige, D. (1988). *Hiding in the light.* New York and London: Routledge.

hooks, b. (1989). *Talking back, thinking feminist, thinking black.* Boston: South End Press.

————. (1990). *Yearning: race, gender and cultural politics.* Boston: South End Press.

James, C. (1993). *Fame in the 20th century.* London: BBC Books.

Jameson, F. (1998). *The cultural turn.* London and New York: Verso.

Katz, E. (1980). Media events: The sense of occasion. *Studies of Visual Communications, 6*(3), 84–89.

Kohn, N. (1994a). Glancing off the postmodern wall: A visit to the making of *Zulu Dawn. Studies in Symbolic Interaction, 16,* 85–106.

————. (1994b). Unjust games: Hollywood as lived metaphor. *Visual Sociology, 9*(1), 52–61.

Krieger, S. (1991). *Social science and the self.* New Brunswick, NJ: Rutgers University Press.

Kroker, A., M. Kroker, and D. Cook. (1989). *Panic encyclopedia: The definitive guide to the postmodern scene.* New York: St. Martin's Press.

Laclau, E., and C. Mouffe. (1985). *Hegemony and socialist strategy.* London and New York: Verso.

Lippmann, W. (1923). *Public Opinion*. New York: Macmillan.

Lyotard, J-F. (1984). *The postmodern condition: A report on knowledge*. Minneapolis: University of Minnesota Press.

———. (1990). *Pacific wall*. (B. Boone, trans.). Venice, CA: Lapis Press.

Margolis, S. (1977). *Fame*. San Francisco: San Francisco Book Company.

McCannell, D. (1992). *Empty meeting grounds*. New York and London: Routledge.

McRobbie, A. (1991). *Feminism and youth culture*. Boston: Unwin Hyman.

Mills, C. W. (1956). *The power elite*. New York: Oxford University Press.

———. (1959). *The sociological imagination*. New York: Oxford University Press.

Nancy, J-L. (1993). *The birth to presence*. Stanford, CA: Stanford University Press.

Neal, P. (1972). *Sport and identity*. Philadelphia: Dorrance & Company.

Olalquiaga, C. (1992). *Megalopolis*. Minneapolis: University of Minnesota Press.

Parker, D. (1994). *The poetry and short stories of Dorothy Parker*. New York: Modern Library.

Perez-Reverte, A. (2004). The queen of the south. (A. Hurley, trans.). New York: Plume.

Pope, A. (1966). *Poetical works*. (H. Davis, ed.). Oxford: Oxford University Press.

Rosaldo, R. (1989). *Culture and truth*. Boston: Beacon Press.

Sansone, D. (1988). *Greek athletics and the genesis of sport*. Berkeley: University of California Press.

Schechner, R. (1985). *Between theater & anthropology*. Philadelphia: University of Pennsylvania Press.

Schickel, R. (1985). *Intimate strangers: The culture of celebrity*. New York: Doubleday & Company.

Sedgwick, E. K. (1992). Epidemics of the will. In J. Crary and S. Kwinter (eds.), *Incorporations* (pp. 582–595). New York: Urzone.

Sennett, R. (1977). *The fall of public man*. New York: Knopf.

Shields, D. (1994). Why we live at the movies. *Utne Reader*, March/April, 170.

Stallybrass, P., and A. White. (1986). *The politics and poetics of transgression*. Ithaca, NY: Cornell University Press.

Stewart, S. (1984). *On longing: Narratives of the miniature, the gigantic, the souvenir, the collection*. Baltimore: Johns Hopkins University Press.

The real mother goose. (1916). Chicago: Rand McNally.

Thompson, J. B. (1990). *Ideology and modern culture*. Cambridge, UK: Polity Press.

Trinh, T. M. (1991). *When the moon waxes red*. New York and London: Routledge.

———. (1989). *Woman, native, other*. Bloomington: University of Indiana Press.

Vattimo, G. (1992). *The transparent society*. (D. Webb, trans.). Baltimore and London: Johns Hopkins University Press.

Virilio, P. (1989). *War and cinema*. (P. Camiller, trans.). London and New York: Verso.

———. (1991). *The aesthetics of disappearance*. (P. Beitchman, trans.). New York: Semiotext(e).

———. (1991). *The lost dimension*. (D. Moshenberg, trans.). New York: Semiotext(e).

———. (1997). *Open sky*. London and New York: Verso.

Visweswaran, K. (1994). *Fictions of feminist ethnography*. Minneapolis: University of Minnesota Press.

Weedon, C. (1987). *Feminist practice and poststructuralist theory*. Cambridge, MA, and Oxford, UK: Blackwell.

Weinstein, D., and M. A. Weinstein. (1991). Georg Simmel: Sociological flaneur bricoleur. *Theory, Culture & Society, 8,* 151–168.

West, C. (1992). Nihilism in black America. In G. Dent (ed.), *Black popular culture* (pp. 37–47). Seattle: Bay Press.

———. (1993). *Prophetic thought in postmodern times*. Monroe, MN: Common Courage Press.

Wordsworth, W. (1959). *The Prelude*. (E. de Selincourt, ed.). Oxford, UK: Clarendon Press.

Young, R. (1990). *White mythologies: writing history and the West*. New York and London: Routledge.

About the Author

Dr. Nathaniel Kohn is an associate professor at the University of Georgia's Grady College of Journalism and Mass Communication, teaching courses in writing for the screen, producing for film and television, cultural studies, and critical theory.

Also at the University of Georgia, Dr. Kohn is associate director of the prestigious George Foster Peabody Awards, considered by many to be the highest award in the electronic media.

Dr. Kohn is festival director of Roger Ebert's Overlooked Film Festival, hosted by *Chicago Sun-Times* film critic Roger Ebert. He also is cofounder and festival director of Robert Osborne's Classic Film Festival.

Dr. Kohn's credits as a motion picture producer include the Sundance Film Festival Selection *Somebodies* and the Academy Award–nominated *Zulu Dawn*, directed by Douglas Hickox and starring Burt Lancaster, Peter O'Toole, John Mills, Simon Sabela, Ken Gampu, and Bob Hoskins. In television, he produced the American version of the award-winning British Channel 4 children's science series *Abracadabra*. He has written commissioned screenplays for companies in Los Angeles, London, Munich, Toronto, Montreal, Zagreb, and Johannesburg and has been a consultant to production companies in Norway, Britain, and Germany. He continues to work as a writer, producer, and consultant to production companies and film festivals.

Dr. Kohn; his wife, Pamela; and his two daughters, Sophie and Lily, live in Athens, Georgia.